PACKED WIT
D0549708
TOP TENS
CHALL NGES
GAMES
PRANKS,
BANTZ &
WHATEV'S

CONTENTS

LIGHTS, CAMERA, ACTION!

YouTube

YouTube has come a long way since the very first video was uploaded to the site in 2005. Nowadays, more people are logging on and watching content than ever before, with over 300 hours of video being uploaded to the site every minute. This is the year that YouTubers have finally been accepted as proper celebrities in the real world; with book deals, TV appearances and millions of fans following their every move. Millions more are being inspired to create their own channels too: shooting, uploading and sharing new videos in an ever-growing creative community.

One thing's for sure – whether we're creating our own content or simply streaming our favouritess, we just love to entertain ourselves with the awesome world of YouTube.

OVER HALF OF US WATCH YOUTUBE ON A SMARTPHONE OR TABLET.

THE YOUTUBE WEBSITE HAS THE MOST VIDEO CONTENT ON THE INTERNET. OVER 300 HOURS OF VIDEO ARE UPLOADED TO THE SITE EVERY MINUTE!

TOGETHER, WE WATCH MORE THAN 6 BILLION HOURS OF YOUTUBE VIDEOS EVERY MONTH.

42% OF INTERNET USERS SAY THEY'VE WATCHED A VLOG IN THE PAST MONTH.

YOUTUBE IS AVAILABLE IN MORE THAN 61 LANGUAGES AND 75 COUNTRIES AROUND THE WORLD.

USERS SPEND AN AVERAGE OF 40 MINUTES PER SESSION WATCHING CONTENT ON MOBILE!

DO YOU KNOW YouTube?

As YouTube has evolved over the years, it's also changed our language and the words we use for things! Whether you're already a fully signed up member of #TeamInternet or new to the YouTube game, you'll never be confused by Internet speak again with our glossary guide to what-means-what on the web.

DID YOU KNOW?
The word YouTuber is now in the official Oxford English Dictionary!

AD: Vloggers must be upfront and clear with audiences when they've been paid to produce content promoting a product, service or brand. Using the word 'ad' in the video title and description signals that a video has been sponsored.

AMA: Stands for 'Ask Me Anything'.

CHALLENGE: A popular trend amongst video creators where participants film themselves competing in various amusing or uncomfortable activities.

CHANNEL: A user's own personal page on YouTube, which shows their uploaded videos, playlists, biography, liked videos and recent activity.

COLLAB: Short for collaboration. This means any type of video where YouTubers appear in each other's videos.

COMMENT: A written response to a video.

COMMUNITY: The name used to describe all the members involved in the YouTube world – creators and fans alike.

DAILY VLOGGER: Someone who video logs their daily life.

DESCRIPTION: The box located underneath the video where YouTubers often leave important links and content relevant to the video.

FANDOMS: The collective name for a group of fans. There are many different fandoms in the YouTube world, each with their own name e.g. Sugglets, Mirfandas, etc.

FAVOURITES: A monthly video breakdown of a YouTuber's favourite items or products.

FEATURED VIDEO: A video that has been selected to automatically play when you click onto a YouTuber's channel page. Often this will be a trailer showcasing what the channel is all about.

GAMER: A YouTuber that makes videos about computer games.

LET'S PLAY: A very popular style of gaming video where viewers watch a YouTuber playing a video game, usually with voice-over commentary.

MEME: An image, activity, video or catchphrase that is copied and spread rapidly from person to person via the Internet, often with slight variations.

PLAYLIST: A collection of videos that can be created using any videos on YouTube. It's a good way of organising content and can also be easily shared with others.

PHANDOM: The fandom name for fans of popular YouTubers Dan and Phil. You are likely to encounter the Phandom if you spend any time at all in the YouTube comments sections.

PRANKSTER: A YouTuber who plays pranks and tricks on family, friends or the public and films their reactions.

Q&A: A simple sit-down question and answer video format used by many YouTubers.

RL: Stands for Real Life. The place that you occasionally have to return to after binge watching YouTube videos for hours.

SHIP: Short for relationship, to 'ship' is to support or endorse a romantic relationship between two people.

SUBSCRIBER: A YouTube user who is subscribed to another user. Subscribers get automatic updates whenever a new video is posted and will also see that channel's activity in their homepage feed.

TAG: A video in which someone completes a themed challenge or set of questions and then 'tags' other people to do them too.

TROLL: A person who deliberately causes controversy in an online setting, and who is best off ignored and reported.

TUTORIAL: A step-by-step guide showing viewers how to do or make something.

THUMBNAILS: A small picture that represents each video on YouTube.

UNBOXING: A hugely popular Internet trend where people film themselves opening or unpacking a new product for the first time.

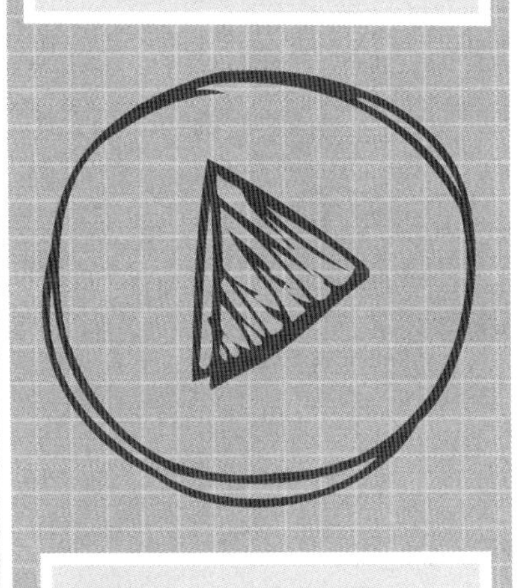

VINE: A social media app where users post short six-second video clips. In October 2016 Vine announced it would be closing. Viners won't be able to post new content, but luckily the website will remain active so we can still enjoy all the hilarious Vines.

VINERS: Someone who uses and uploads to the Vine app. There is some crossover between Viners and YouTubers, as more and more Viners begin to use YouTube too.

VIRAL: A piece of content (YouTube video, Vine, blog article, photo, etc.) that has rapidly become very popular. This often occurs thanks to word of mouth and the frequent sharing of one particular piece of content all over the Internet.

VLOG: Video blog. A conversational video format featuring a person talking directly to camera.

VLOGGER: Any individual who documents their life, thoughts, opinions and interests in video form on YouTube.

VLOGMAS: The time of year where YouTubers take on the challenge of vlogging and uploading festive footage every day in the run-up to Christmas Day.

YOUTUBE: The most popular video-sharing site on the web.

YOUTUBER: A frequent user of the YouTube website, particularly someone who produces and appears in videos for the purpose of entertaining or informing others. YouTubers can span from comedians to gamers, musicians to vloggers… read on to discover more of the most popular types of YouTuber in this book!

ROFLMAO

Comedy is one of the most popular categories on YouTube, and with so many funny people to choose from there's bound to be a channel guaranteed to give you the giggles. Online comedians all have their own distinct brand of humour, from skits and stand-up to downright silliness – here are just some of the types of comedy vlogs you'll find for lots of LOLs.

FAILS

>>>>>>

One of the earliest types of YouTube comedy channel were those dedicated to posting all things fail. From crazy cats and funny babies to a whole lot of people falling flat on their faces, these videos capture the most epic RL fails that we can't help but laugh at.

JUST LIKE: FailArmy, JukinVideo, Break

SKITS AND SKETCHES

>>>>>>>>>>>>>

Who needs TV comedies with all the innovative skits and sketches YouTubers have to offer! Skits are generally shorter, non-scripted and improvisational, whereas sketches are usually pre-planned with a script, a cast of characters and props and costumes. From real-life situations to the absolutely absurd, both types of video offer original and funny ideas and lots of opportunity for goofing around.

JUST LIKE: 5secondfilms, CollegeHumor, Smosh, ForSkitsAndGiggles

RANTS

>>>>>>>>>>>>>

Sometimes YouTubers will go off on a bit of a 'rant' on screen, offering their witty takes on topics we can all relate to. This kind of observational comedy pokes fun at the humorous aspects of everyday life by pointing out the silly things which we all accept as normal, but can also be used to highlight important issues too.

JUST LIKE: nigahiga, danisnotonfire, JennaMarbles

IMPRESSIONS

>>>>>>>>>>>>>

From imitating movie stars and TV characters to singers, animals and even other YouTubers, these impersonators do their best to make us laugh by copying other people to perfection.

JUST LIKE: ThatcherJoe, Noodlerella, Mikey Bolts

ALTER EGOS AND CHARACTERS

>>>>>>>>>>>>>

Some YouTube comedians like to breathe life into their own original characters and they make appearances in videos on the regs. With their distinct personalities, costumes and hilarious antics, we get to know these characters almost as well as the stars behind them!

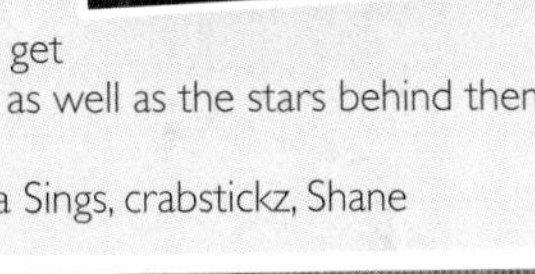

JUST LIKE: IISuperwomanII, Miranda Sings, crabstickz, Shane

PARODIES

>>>>>>>>>>>

YouTube is the place to go for hilarious parodies, which imitate and put an amusing spin on everything in pop culture; such as music, movies and video games. From iconic pop songs to Apple adverts, there's nothing these stars won't poke fun at.

JUST LIKE: Bart Baker, jacksfilms, The Key of Awesome

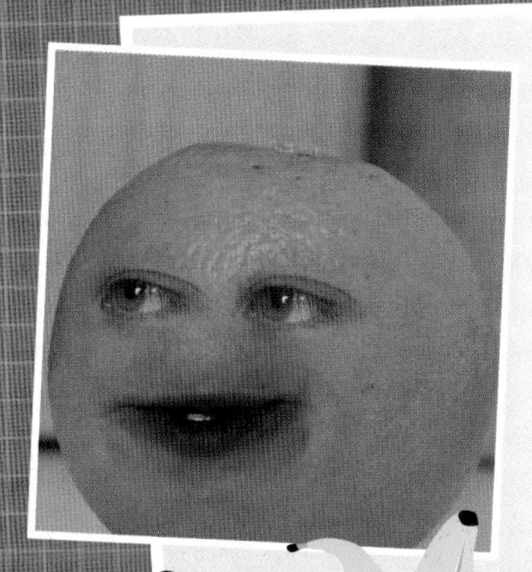

SLAPSTICK

>>>>>>>>>>>>>

Slapstick comedy is purely physical – from tripping and slipping over to rough-and-tumble, dropping things and spilling stuff – nothing makes us laugh more than some good old-fashioned silliness. And with these channels, the sillier the better!

JUST LIKE: Annoying Orange, Just For Laughs Gags, Mr. Bean

BEST IN BLOOPERS

Another comedy staple on YouTube is the classic blooper video, where Internet stars keep all the funny moments, mess-ups and mistakes they've made and upload them for our entertainment. It's not just the comedy stars who have cottoned on to keeping the bloopers in either – everyone's at it! Check out the very best bloopers from our favourite web celebs.

SOME BLOOPERS FROM PHIL IS NOT ON FIRE 6 – DANISNOTINTERESTING

>>>>>>>>>>>>>>>>>>>>>>>>>>>>

Dan and Phil know how to give the fans what they what – even more Dan and Phil! This video shows the pair being doubly hilarious as they crack each other up in bloopers from a classic 'phil is not on fire' upload.

BLOOPERS: HOW ANIMALS EAT THEIR FOOD – MISTEREPICMANN2

>>>>>>>>>>>>>>>>>>>>>>>>>>>>

Unless you've been living under a WiFi-free rock, you've probably already seen the hilarious viral video 'How Animals Eat Their Food' (if you haven't, go watch it now!). This video lets us see the bloopers from the making of the original video, and to be honest, we think it might even be funnier than the first!

YOUTUBER WHISPERS 4 – BLOOPERS & EXTRAS – THATCHERJOEVLOGS

>>>>>>>>>>>>>>>>>>>>>>>>>>>>

Maybe turn down the volume a bit for this one. It's got four of our favourites: Louise, Dan, Phil, Joe, and a whole lot of SHOUTING.

THE BOYFRIEND TAG BLOOPERS – EXTRATYLER

>>>>>>>>>>>>>>>>>

The video that won a Teen Choice Award for "Best Collaboration" and spawned the Troyler fandom has bloopers! Extra Troye and Tyler? We'll take it.

KEEP IT IN

If you're making your own YouTube videos, why not try including your blooper moments at the end of your videos to keep viewers entertained until the very last second. Bloopers are almost always funny, as demonstrated by popular YouTubers like Zoella and nigahiga.

MIRANDA BLOOPERS – PSYCHOSOPRANO

>>>>>>>>>>>>>>>>>>>>>>>>>>>

It seems that whenever Miranda Sings does a collab video, no one around her can keep a straight face. We love seeing the behind-the-scenes moments when it all gets too much for even Colleen and she temporarily breaks character for a good old giggle. Wait, you didn't know Miranda Sings was a character? Soz – laugh it off by watching this hilarious bloopers vid.

SOME OF THE BIG YOUTUBERS HAVE EXTRA CHANNELS JUST FOR POSTING THEIR BLOOPER VIDEOS!

SIBLING TAG BLOOPERS & EXTRAS – THATCHERJOEVLOGS

>>>>>>>>>>>>>>>>>>>>>>>>>>>

Zoë and Joe give us all of the sibling goals and giggles in a bloopers video longer than the actual sibling tag they filmed.

TOP 10 COMEDIANS

If you're in need of a good laugh, these top comedy channels provide them by the barrel full; with more parodies, sketches and silliness than you can shake a stick at!

#10 MIRANDA SINGS

AKA: Colleen Ballinger
ON YT SINCE: January 2008
KNOWN FOR: Comically talentless singing, dancing and terrible advice.

Miranda Sings is the self-obsessed, wannabe pop star parody of a person created by comedian Colleen Ballinger. She gives terrible make-up tutorials, hits back at her 'haters', sings badly and dances terribly – but we all somehow still love her anyway!

SUBSCRIBERS • 7.3 MILLION

Miranda has her own TV show called 'Haters Back Off!'

#9 SHANE

AKA: Shane Yaw
ON YT SINCE: September 2005
KNOWN FOR: Hilarious sketches, songs, impersonations and music video spoofs.

Shane Dawson's millions of fans flock to his three YouTube channels for outrageous comedy videos packed full of crazy Internet commentaries, music video parodies and original comedy songs. Shane's also known for his funny sketches featuring colourful characters such as Shanaynay, Fefe Fierce, Ned the Nerd and Aunt Hilda.

SUBSCRIBERS • 8.6 MILLION

#8 IISUPERWOMANII

AKA: Lilly Singh
ON YT SINCE: October 2010
KNOWN FOR: Observational comedy, sketches and dressing up as her over-protective 'parents'!

Talented Lilly Singh is a vlogger, singer, rapper, actress and motivational speaker who tackles everything on her YT channel. No topic is too big, too small or too controversial for this superwoman, and she's great at putting a funny spin on common issues that we all face; from parent troubles to social media stresses.

Almost all of Lilly's sketches are based on people she knows in real life!

#7 RAY WILLIAM JOHNSON

AKA: Ray William Johnson

ON YT SINCE: May 2008

KNOWN FOR: Sarcastic reviews of viral vids and other comedy series.

Ray William Johnson shot to fame with his 'Equals Three' show, which was the first channel of its kind, providing hilarious commentaries on popular viral videos. These days Ray doesn't do it all himself, but is still going strong with a whole team of hosts producing some of the best comedy shows on the web.

Johnson's was the first ever YouTube channel to reach 5 million subscribers, back in 2011.

#6 COLLEGEHUMOR

AKA: A whole team of comedians

ON YT SINCE: October 2006

KNOWN FOR: Hilarious high-quality sketches, animations and web series.

If you haven't already heard of CollegeHumor, where have you been? Head to the channel to check out popular series like 'Jake and Amir' and 'Hardly Working' and stay for some of the sharpest comedy on YouTube, with a huge selection of original sketches and videos spanning all sorts of subjects.

SUBSCRIBERS +11.3 MILLION

#5 GOOD MYTHICAL MORNING

AKA: Rhett McLaughlin and Charles Lincoln

ON YT SINCE: September 2008

KNOWN FOR: A daily morning talk show format featuring fun, games and hilarious yet informative facts.

Rhett and Link have been best friends since their first year of school, and the laughs haven't stopped since! On their YouTube morning talk show, the duo compete in hilarious games and challenges, tackle disgusting taste tests, share stories and teach you everything you never thought you wanted to know; from five facts about bellybuttons to the weird things you can do with duct tape!

SUBSCRIBERS +11.5 MILLION

GMM is actually Rhett and Link's second YouTube channel, which became more popular than the first! It's now the most watched daily show online.

#4 FINE BROTHERS ENTERTAINMENT

AKA: Benny and Rafi Fine
ON YT SINCE: June 2007
KNOWN FOR: React videos and scripted sketches.

SUBSCRIBERS • 14.6 MILLION

Brothers Benny and Rafi had been in the video making business for years before hitting Internet gold with their 'REACT' YouTube series, resulting in several awards and a huge online empire. Their videos include kid's, teen's, adult's, YouTuber's and elder's reactions to all kinds of weird and wonderful things on the web, as well as comedy series like 'Emo Dad' and original sketches too.

#3 JENNAMARBLES

AKA: Jenna Mourey
ON YT SINCE: February 2010
KNOWN FOR: Her hilarious, honest skits, relatable rants and cute pooches.

SUBSCRIBERS • 16.6 MILLION

Jenna shot to viral YouTube fame with her video, 'How to trick people into thinking you're good looking', and is now the funniest female on the site! Jenna takes simple truths about girls and guys and turns them into comedy gold, offers hilarious make-up tips and covers all kinds of topics in her energetic rants.

#2 NIGAHIGA

AKA: Ryan Higa
ON YT SINCE: July 2006
KNOWN FOR: Spoofs, rants, sketches, music videos and vlogs.

Ryan Higa has come a long way since his early lip-syncing uploads way back in 2006 and is now widely adored for his fast-paced comic delivery, amazing creativity and heavily edited vids. From hilarious how-to guides to slick sketches, music parodies, dares and 'Dear Ryan' fan suggestions, this comedy star's channel will leave you laughing for hours.

Ryan has over 3 BILLION video views!

"SHUT UP!"

#1 SMOSH

>>>>>>>>>>>>>>>>>>>>>>>>>>

SUBSCRIBERS

+ 22.4 MILLION

AKA: Anthony Padilla and Ian Hecox

ON YT SINCE: November 2005

KNOWN FOR: Scripted sketches, video-game themed music videos, improvisations, movie spoofs and a whole lot of silliness!

Best friends Ian and Anthony first met at school, where they quickly discovered their knack for making people laugh. The pair were among the earliest comedy pioneers on YouTube, after starting their journey way back in 2005 with a hilarious video of them lip-syncing to the Pokémon theme tune. Since then, Smosh has reached new levels of popularity and entertainment, with the boys branching out to include their truly bonkers sketches, food battles, crazy costumes, spoof songs, improvisations and wacky challenges. Fans can't get enough of their unique brand of unpredictable but harmless humour, and these days the team has expanded to bring us even more Smoshy goodness, with multiple channels including gaming, animations, other languages and even more funny people!

The funny pair have even starred in their own feature length film, 'Smosh: The Movie', alongside several other big YouTube names.

Smosh has been the #1 most subscribed channel on YouTube on three separate occasions.

WATCH: POKEMON IN REAL LIFE!

This classic video from six years ago has over 50 million views. Did these two actually predict Pokémon GO?!

A lot of planning and resources goes into the making of a Smosh video. Apparently, it takes about two weeks to make a complex three to five minute long Smosh video, including the filming, editing and producing.

IF YOU LIKE THESE, YOU'LL LOVE...

BLIMEY COW

BART BAKER

JACKSFILMS

JACK MAYNARD

ONE TO WATCH: THETHIRDPEW

KNOCK KNOCK...

COULD YOU BE THE NEXT COMEDY STAR?

If you're known as the class clown or you're always the one making your mates laugh, you might want to consider starting your own comedy channel! The Internet is the perfect platform for sketch comedians to stand up and get noticed, so read on for top tips on how you can get started.

"The main thing is that you post videos that people want to see; majority of the time, it's comedy. Once you find your own style that works for you, you must continuously produce and post videos. Personally, I always watch my own videos as if I were the audience, before I post them. If it's something I think they'll enjoy and won't be offended by, it's good to go!"
– Ryan Higa

FIND YOUR STYLE

Are you great at celeb impressions, or known to make your mates howl with some slapstick humour? Find out what type of comedy you're best at, and make this the focus of your comedy videos. Many YouTube comedy stars started off doing something completely different, so don't stress too much if you can't figure it out straight away – experiment with different styles instead.

ASK A FRIEND

If you're not sure about an idea, try it out on a friend first to see if it makes them laugh. Their feedback could help to make your jokes even funnier! You could even get your mates involved in filming the videos too by creating funny sketches with a whole cast of characters.

Smosh's Anthony and Ian always discuss and work on ideas together to make them as funny as they can be before turning them into a script.

MAKE VIDEOS THAT YOU'D FIND FUNNY

There's no one type of comedy video that will appeal to everyone, because everyone has a different sense of humour. Try to make videos that you find funny and hopefully you'll find others who will laugh along too!

GET DRESSED UP

Using props and costumes to get into character can really help improve the quality and look of your videos.

WATCH LOTS OF YOUTUBE!

Get inspiration from watching other YouTubers who never fail to make you laugh. This is a great way to learn about things like comic timing and style. Don't just copy others though and definitely don't steal their jokes – figure out what makes them funny and use that to find your own original comedy style.

"Pick something topical, pick something universal, pick something that anybody watching knows." – Rafi Fine

"I take stuff from my everyday life. Like, once I was bitten by a squirrel and I thought, "well, there's a video!" – Phil Lester

DO SOMETHING UNEXPECTED

Take inspiration from the everyday, ordinary things around you and figure out how to put an unexpected spin on it that makes it funny.

TELL STORIES

Have a funny story about something that's happened to you in real life? Why not make it into a video!

BE RELATABLE

Everyone likes to watch comedy that they can relate to. Comedians like JennaMarbles often tell humorous but relatable real life stories that connect with their audiences.

DON'T BE OFFENSIVE

Making fun of people or using offensive jokes in comedy videos may get some attention, but for all the wrong reasons.

WRITE A SCRIPT

If you're making a comedy sketch, it's important to write a script first so you know what's going to happen and where the jokes are. Make sure you rehearse too so it looks seamless when the time comes to film it.

You're never too young to be funny!

Zay Zay Fredericks started his channel aged just six years old and he now has over 70k subscribers!

START PLANNING YOUR OWN COMEDY SKETCH HERE!

RL EVENTS

Several times a year, vlogging stars step out from behind their cameras and onto a stage at exciting fan events that take place all over the world. So, if you fancy seeing your fave YouTubers in the flesh, get these digital event dates in your diary, stat!

SUMMER IN THE CITY

WHEN: August

WHERE: ExCel Centre, London

WHAT: The UK's largest annual YouTube event. With loads of top YouTube creators, live performances, panels, meet-and-greets and merch, it's a must-visit for any UK-based vlogging fan.

AMITY FEST

WHEN: TBC

WHERE: Touring the UK

WHAT: The British YouTube super crew on tour. You'll get to see the likes of Zoella, Alfie, Louise and Tanya in various locations around the UK as they strut their stuff on stage.

BUFFER FESTIVAL

WHEN: Autumn

WHERE: Toronto, Canada

WHAT: YouTube's answer to the Cannes Film Festival. Creative content makers from across the world join together to celebrate and showcase their stuff on the big screen in front of an audience.

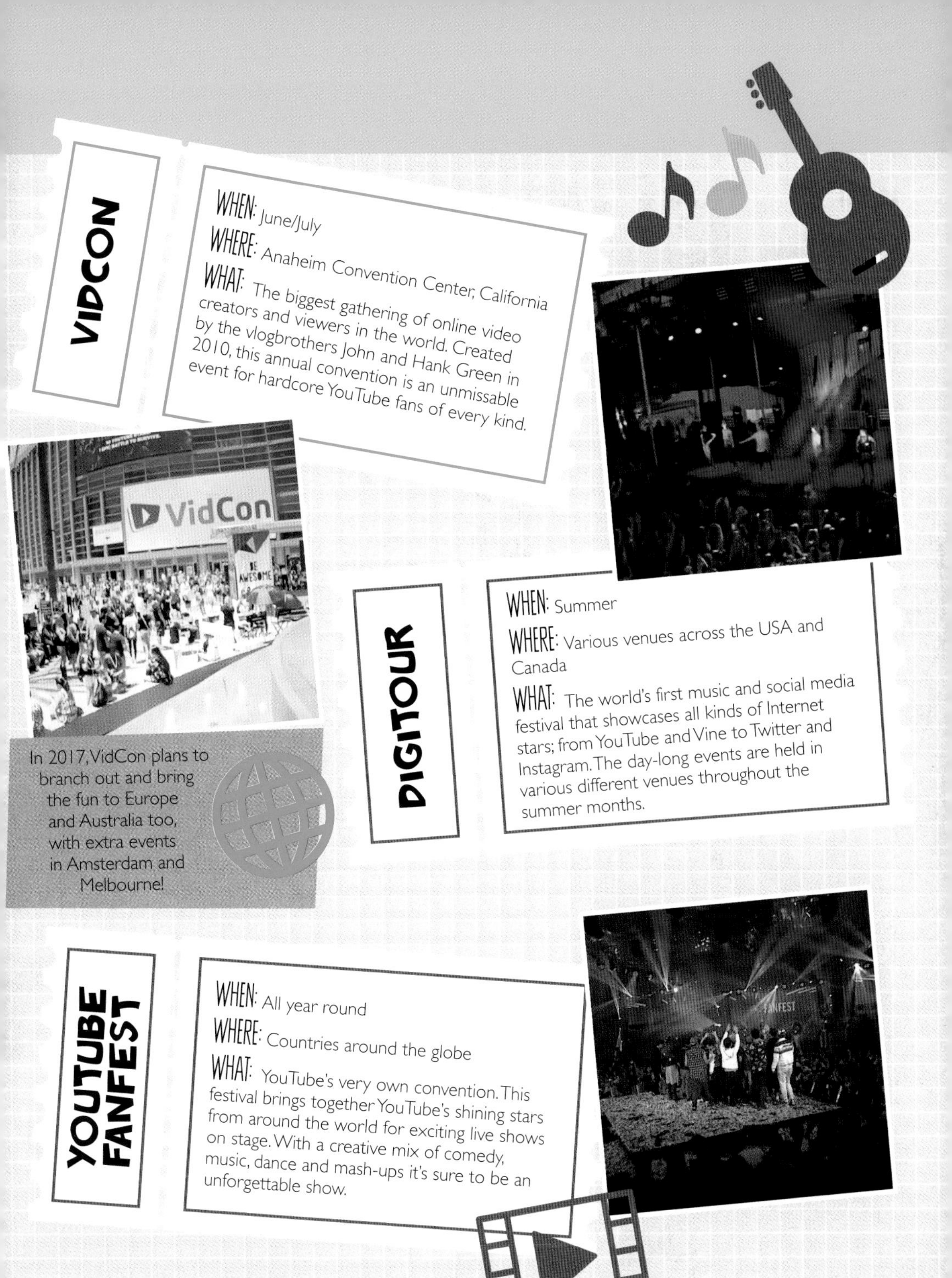

VIDCON

WHEN: June/July

WHERE: Anaheim Convention Center, California

WHAT: The biggest gathering of online video creators and viewers in the world. Created by the vlogbrothers John and Hank Green in 2010, this annual convention is an unmissable event for hardcore YouTube fans of every kind.

In 2017, VidCon plans to branch out and bring the fun to Europe and Australia too, with extra events in Amsterdam and Melbourne!

DIGITOUR

WHEN: Summer

WHERE: Various venues across the USA and Canada

WHAT: The world's first music and social media festival that showcases all kinds of Internet stars; from YouTube and Vine to Twitter and Instagram. The day-long events are held in various different venues throughout the summer months.

YOUTUBE FANFEST

WHEN: All year round

WHERE: Countries around the globe

WHAT: YouTube's very own convention. This festival brings together YouTube's shining stars from around the world for exciting live shows on stage. With a creative mix of comedy, music, dance and mash-ups it's sure to be an unforgettable show.

PLAYLIST LIVE

WHEN: Twice a year

WHERE: Orlando, Florida and Washington D.C.

WHAT: One huge YouTube and Vine meet-up. Based in the U.S., Playlist Live is one of the best events to be able to meet Internet creators in real life, with meet-and-greets, interactive panels and live shows galore.

BEAUTYCON

WHEN: Dates throughout the year

WHERE: Various locations

WHAT: Beautycon brings together the best beauty gurus from YouTube, Instagram, Snapchat and Vine. The day-long event has so far taken place in stylish cities such as L.A., New York and London, where creators, stars, fans and beauty and lifestyle brands all gather for tutorials, panels, live music and meet-ups.

AMPLIFY LIVE

WHEN: Spring

WHERE: Touring Australia and New Zealand

WHAT: A live show featuring some of the world's biggest YouTube and music stars. The launch of Amplify Live in 2015 meant Aussie YouTube fans no longer need to miss out on awesome live events.

WHEN: September

WHERE: The NEC, Birmingham

WHAT: The UK's biggest gaming convention. EGX offers gaming fans the opportunity to meet YouTube stars such as Tom Cassell, check out and play new games, cosplay, learn from developers and experience eSports live.

WHEN: June

WHERE: Los Angeles Convention Center, California

WHAT: E3 is the biggest event in the video games industry. It's a must-see for many gamers since it showcases exciting new technology and never-before-seen products and games.

Though the annual event is typically only for journalists, industry officials and investors, thanks to YouTube Gaming, viewers around the world can get front-row E3 access with trailers, talks, exclusive live Let's Plays' and streaming with some of YouTube's biggest gamers, like Rooster Teeth, iHasCupquake and CaptainSparklez.

AWARDS!

You can also catch your favourite Team Internet and social media stars at these top award shows held throughout the year. Why not nominate your faves for an award and vote for them to win!

PRANKS FOR WATCHING!

Can you believe that some people get paid to prank for a living? Whether you like them or loathe them, YouTube pranks are now incredibly popular, with entire channels dedicated to pranking and new videos going viral every week.

Top content creators plan, set-up and pull off all kinds of elaborate pranks on friends, family and unsuspecting members of the public. Here are just some of the hilarious ways they do it!

HIDDEN CAMERAS

>>>>>>>>>>>>

Pranks are only really funny when the person's reaction is genuine, so most pranks are filmed using hidden camera set-ups so the subjects don't suspect a thing. Sometimes the best part of a prank is when we see pranksters show their 'victims' the hidden camera and they can laugh it off together at the end.

JUST LIKE: Just For Laughs Gags

PRANK CALLS

>>>>>>

Armed with nothing but a phone and an arsenal of silly voices, these jokers dial everyone from their parents to strangers and record the calls for our entertainment. It's one of the simplest pranks in the book so pretty much anyone can try and pull it off!

JUST LIKE: Ownage Pranks

SCARY PRANKS

>>>>>>>>>>>>

From flesh-eating zombies to giant spiders, freaky masks and fake blood, these pranks are all about using scary set-ups to give people the fright of their lives. Some of them are like scenes from a horror movie in real life!

JUST LIKE: DmPranksProductions

REVENGE PRANKS

>>>>>>>>>>>>

These are pranks carried out on fellow practical jokers instead of the public, where two or more pranksters try to get revenge on each other for previous pranks pulled. These pranks can continue for months or even years and get bigger and better as each prankster tries to one-up the other! Viewers love to check in to see who's winning the prank wars.

JUST LIKE: PrankvsPrank

PROP PRANKS

>>>>>>>>>>>>

From fake snakes to crazy costumes and disguises, these pranksters use creative props to pull off their pranks. Costumes and props often reflect the theme of the pranks and either help to make them more believable or just add to the fun if they're already far fetched!

JUST LIKE: Rémi GAILLARD

AWKWARD PRANKS

>>>>>>>>>>>>

Some YouTubers pull pranks that are painfully cringeworthy, but still somehow entertaining to watch. These pranksters go out of their way to create super awkward situations; from farting in public to uncomfortable conversations, and you've got to admire their guts.

JUST LIKE: LAHWF

WARNING

Always think before you prank – there can be serious consequences, whether that's putting yourself or somebody else in danger or actually breaking the law. Though you might see some crazy pranks online, what many viewers don't realise is that pranks have often been set-up in advance with willing participants. Pranks should always stay firmly on the funny side and not be designed to distress, humiliate or make fun of others.

MAGICAL PRANKS

>>>>>>>>>>>>

These talented pranksters incorporate elements of magic into their pranks to leave people feeling amazed instead of annoyed. From invisibility stunts to mind readers and making money appear from thin air, there are plenty of jaw-dropping jokes online.

JUST LIKE: MagicofRahat

"IT'S JUST A PRANK, BRO!"

Fool your friends and family with these funny pranks to try out at home. Just don't forget to record their reactions!

THE SNAKE PRANK

>>>>>>>>>>>>>>>>>>>>>>>>>>>>>>

This classic prank is the perfect stunt to pull during school lunch breaks. To pull it off, you'll need a plastic toy snake with a length of fishing line tied around it's head. Tie a bulldog clip to the other end of the line and then clip it to your friend's shoelaces or backpack. When they get up to walk somewhere, yell out "OMG there's a snake!" and watch as they freak out with the snake following!

THE SHOWER PRANK

>>>>>>>>>>>>>>>>

Baffle your family by preparing this bathroom prank. Take a small piece of cling film and unscrew the top of the bottles you want to mess with – it could be the shampoo, shower gel or both! Put the cling film across the top of the bottle and make sure you trim it with scissors so you can't see any poking out before putting the caps back on. Your unsuspecting victims will be left in the shower wondering why they can't get anything out!

THE OREO PRANK

>>>>>>>>>>>>>>>>>>>>>>>>>>>>>>

This is a fun and easy trick to try any time. First, take an Oreo cookie apart and use a butter knife to scrape out the white filling. Replace the filling with white minty toothpaste and squeeze the top back on. Finally, put the Oreos back into the packet and offer them around to your unsuspecting mates!

THE CLOCK PRANK

Want to wind up one of your family members? Take all the alarm clocks in the house and set them for the same time. Next hide them around the person's room in lots of different places. When the time comes for the alarms to go off they'll hear noises coming from everywhere and – most annoyingly – the clocks will keep going off until they manage to find them all!

THE MAYO PRANK

This cool trick will totally gross everyone out! Take an old empty mayonnaise jar (make sure the label is still on) and fill it with vanilla yoghurt. Take the mayonnaise jar out the fridge when your family are around and start eating straight out of it with a spoon. Or, take the jar to school and get it out at lunch in front of your friends – why not try offering it around, too!

THE PHONE PRANK

'Borrow' your friend's phone and create some shortcuts. You could change 'LOL' to autocorrect to 'lots of love' or 'and' to 'monkey'. For an extra prank update your contact name to read 'Mum', then send them messages, pretending to be their doting mother.

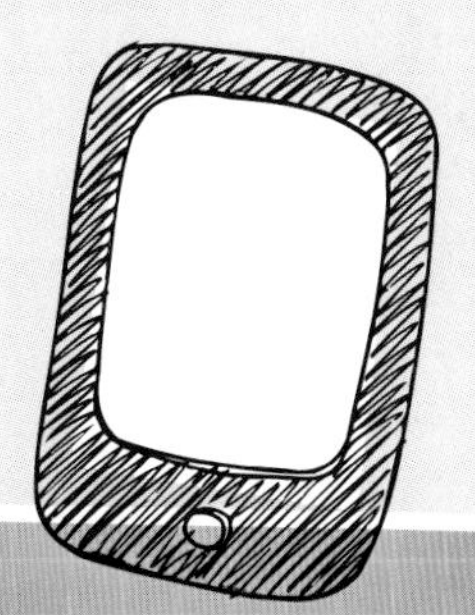

>> >> TOP 10 << <<
PRANKSTERS

Every day is April Fools' Day for YouTube's top pranksters, who are on a mission to make viewers cringe and crack up in any way they can. Check out the 10 best mischief-makers regularly racking up millions of views for their outrageously funny stunts.

#10 ED BASSMASTER

>>>>>>>>>>>>>>>>

AKA: Edwin Rodriguez
ON YT SINCE: September 2006
KNOWN FOR: Crazily cringeworthy character pranks.

SUBSCRIBERS + 2 MILLION

If you like your pranks to be as goofy and awkward as possible, then this is the channel for you. Ed Bassmaster is all about dressing up, donning wigs and doing pranks as one of his original characters, and it's his constant commitment to the roles that really make his channel so fun to watch. Whether Ed's acting as Emilio, Skippy or Mumbles, he loves to use his characters to mess with people to the max.

"Would ya look at this!"

WATCH: 'Drive Thru Invisible Driver Prank'

#9 OWNAGE PRANKS

>>>>>>>>>>>>

AKA: Unknown
ON YT SINCE: August 2007
KNOWN FOR: The funniest prank calls on YouTube.

SUBSCRIBERS + 4.1 MILLION

Ownage Pranks is a talented voice actor who takes prank calling to a whole new level on his hilarious channel. Ownage has never revealed his own face or name, but instead plays the role of a mix of original characters, using a variety of voices and accents to cause maximum mischief whenever his target picks up the phone!

#8 MAGICOFRAHAT

>>>>>>>>>>>>>>>>>>>>>>>>>>

AKA: Rahat Hossain
ON YT SINCE: July 2007
KNOWN FOR: Elaborate pranks, creative set-ups and magic.

SUBSCRIBERS + 4.7 MILLION

MagicofRahat is not your typical YouTube prankster. Instead of trying to wind people up, he pulls off pranks like you've never seen before by incorporating elements of magic with elaborate set-ups to surprise and amaze his unsuspecting victims. Rahat is best known for his creative drive thru pranks where he shocks employees with seemingly impossible scenarios, from invisible drivers to floating drinks cups!

#7 RÉMI GAILLARD

AKA: Rémi Gaillard

ON YT SINCE: July 2007

KNOWN FOR: Dangerously funny videos and pop culture pranks.

Rémi GAILLARD is one of the original YouTube pranksters and also one of the best. Known all over the world for his daring pranks on members of the public and even the police, there's no prank this French mischief-maker won't try to pull off. From real life Mario Kart on the roads and playing Pacman in a supermarket to dressing up in animal costumes and showing off his sports skills, Remi's pranks and antics provide viewers with hours of entertainment.

SUBSCRIBERS + 5.9 MILLION

#6 CASPAR

AKA: Caspar Lee

ON YT SINCE: November 2011

KNOWN FOR: Pranks, challenges and general joking around.

Cheeky chappy Caspar Lee is the South African YouTube star kidding his way to global domination. When he's not entertaining viewers with his good-natured humour or pulling cringe-inducing pranks on his mates or his mum, Caspar can be found interviewing A-list stars, starring in movies and TV shows, writing scripts, and performing stand-up comedy.

SUBSCRIBERS + 6.9 MILLION

#5 THATCHERJOE

AKA: Joe Sugg

ON YT SINCE: November 2011

KNOWN FOR: Impressions, collabs and inventive pranks – often on BFF Caspar Lee.

Joe Sugg loves nothing more than to make a fool out of himself on camera for our entertainment. His fun channel is packed with practical jokes featuring roommate revenge videos, mousetraps, tin foil, balloons, prank calls and a whole lot of post-it notes. Besides his hilarious pranks, Joe is loved by fans for his unique impressions, goofy personality and always-inventive video ideas.

SUBSCRIBERS + 7.6 MILLION

"Of all the videos I've done on ThatcherJoe, my favourites have to be the pranks!"

Vitaly hit the big screen in 2016 with 'Natural Born Pranksters' – a movie he made with pals and fellow prankers Roman Atwood and Dennis Roady.

#4 VITALYZDTV

>>>>>>>>>>>>>

AKA: Vitaly Zdorovetskiy

ON YT SINCE: August 2011

KNOWN FOR: Edgy prank videos and pranks gone wrong.

SUBSCRIBERS • 9.2 MILLION

Russian prankster Vitaly Zdorovetskiy pulls some of the most outrageous pranks out there and is not afraid to face the consequences. When he's not scaring everyone in sight with zombie prank attacks or pretend chainsaw massacres, he's putting his subjects in some very awkward situations and filming their reactions. Vitaly lets subscribers see the prank reactions that didn't go quite according to plan, which often result in a lot of running away.

#3 FOUSEYTUBE

>>>>>>>>>>>>>>>>>>>>>>>>>>

AKA: Yousef Erakat

SUBSCRIBERS • 9.7 MILLION

ON YT SINCE: March 2011

KNOWN FOR: Good-natured pranks, thought provoking experiments and the funniest laugh on YT.

Palestinian-American YouTuber Yousef Erakat, aka fouseyTUBE, first started out making sketches on YouTube but became even more popular with the introduction of his epic prank videos. Fousey's been pranking people ever since and is never short of new and exciting ideas to keep his 9 million subscribers laughing. Popular uploads include prank wars, thought-provoking social experiments and feel good pranks such as the huge viral hit 'SPIDERMAN IN REAL LIFE PRANK!', which has over 130 million views!

#2 ROMANATWOOD

>>>>>>>>>>>>>>

AKA: Roman Atwood

ON YT SINCE: November 2009

KNOWN FOR: Over-the-top antics, risky hidden camera pranks and daily vlogs.

Roman Atwood is the notorious hidden camera prankster known for his uncanny ability to annoy other people and push his luck with his crazy stunts. Roman's pranking subjects range from members of the public to friends, neighbours, fellow pranksters and his girlfriend; who famously gave the joker a taste of his own medicine in his most popular video: 'Anniversary Prank Backfires!!' Despite his huge YouTube fame, Roman still manages to pull off original stunts on a major scale, from giant ball pit pranks to covering an entire house in toilet paper!

Almost every one of Roman's prank videos have gone viral, regularly racking up millions of views each!

SUBSCRIBERS

• 10.1 MILLION

#1 PRANKVSPRANK

>>>>>>>>>>>>>>>>>>>>>>>>>

SUBSCRIBERS

+10.2 MILLION

AKA: Jesse Wellens and Jeana Smith

ON YT SINCE: November 2009

KNOWN FOR: YouTube's original pranking couple playing elaborate revenge pranks on each other.

Former bf and gf Jesse and Jeana are YouTube's most popular pranking duo. The famous couple first started their PrankvsPrank channel back in 2009 when Jesse decided to play a scare prank on Jeana and filmed her reaction. The pair have been wrapped up in an ongoing prank war ever since, each of them trying to outdo the other and take their pranks to the next level! Their series of funny and original pranks and tricks have launched Jesse and Jeana to Internet fame and fortune, with over 10 million subscribers and 1.8 billion views. When they're weren't busy tormenting each other the couple turned their attention to bigger pranks on the public and teamed up with other YouTube stars too. Jesse and Jeana may no longer be boyfriend vs. girlfriend, but the pranks and bants are sure to continue on their channel, with projects like their original 'Prank Academy' series promising to deliver a ridiculous amount of laughs.

Jesse and Jeana's second YouTube channel, BFvsGF, also has a whopping 9 million subscribers.

In 2015 PrankvsPrank received a Streamy Award for the Best Prank Series.

FIRST EVER PRANK: 'GIRLFRIEND FAKE HEAD IN BED SCARE PRANK' – 16.9 million views.

These two were pranking each other long before YouTube – Jeana even pranked Jesse on their first date!

IF YOU LIKE THESE, YOU'LL LOVE...

MEDIOCREFILMS

IMPROV EVERYWHERE

BIGDAWSTV

STUART EDGE

ONE TO WATCH: ROB ANDERSON

PRANK WARS

JOE'S SNEAKY TIP: TIMING

"It's all about the right timing, so you've got to wait a little while before pranking them again."

Best friends Joe Sugg and Caspar Lee, aka 'Jaspar', are well known for the epically hilarious pranks they play on other, which began when they were roommates and keep getting bigger and better! But who is your winner in the ultimate prank wars – Team Caspar or Team Joe?

1 TEAM CASPAR

TEAM CASPAR: 'BREAKING UP WITH MY ROOMMATE FT. THATCHERJOE'

It all started in June 2014, when Caspar decided to play a prank call on his then roommate Joe, pretending he didn't want to live with him anymore. Caspar's prank is halfway between hilarious and heartbreaking as Joe genuinely looks close to tears! But he soon got over it and started plotting the ultimate revenge…

TEAM JOE 2

TEAM JOE: 'ULTIMATE ROOMMATE REVENGE PRANKS'

…With a whole WEEK of pranks! With five pranks for the price of one, this video features a whole lot of hard work from Joe and hilarious reactions from Caspar. From the classic cling film over the toilet prank to jumping out of a cupboard and terrifying Caspar to covering his room in Post-its and cups of water, this has got to be one of the best prank vids of all time.

3 TEAM CASPAR

TEAM CASPAR: 'GIRLFRIEND PRANKS MY ROOMMATE'

How did Caspar get revenge for Joe's epic week of pranks? By hiring an actress to pretend to be his girlfriend, of course. Caspar secretly films what happens when his 'girlfriend' hits on Joe when he leaves the room, and the cringe level is almost too much to handle!

4 TEAM JOE

TEAM JOE: 'ULTIMATE BALLOON PRANK ON MY ROOMATE'

Poor old Joe soon manages to get his own back, Sugg-style. After spending an entire night blowing up over 1,000 balloons, Joe filled Caspar's room with them and hid fellow joker Oli White in the middle of the room dressed as a scary clown. The time-consuming double prank paid off when Caspar got the absolute fright of his life!

CASPAR'S SNEAKY TIP: USE PROPS

"My favourite prop is my mum, because you'd never expect her to be pranking someone."

5 TEAM CASPAR

TEAM CASPAR: 'ROOMMATE SHOWER PRANK'

Next, Caspar comes up with a plan to mess with Joe's precious shower time. He tests out a variety of shower pranks, including covering Joe's towel in red food dye to make him look 'redder than an embarrassed lobster', making the shower run freezing cold and even leaving a stink bomb in the bathroom – all resulting in one very unhappy roommate.

6 TEAM JOE

TEAM JOE: 'NO SLEEP FOR ROOMMATE PRANK'

Caspar loves his sleep even more than he loves pizza, so Joe decided to hit him where it hurts and pull off the classic alarm clock prank (see page 25)! Over the course of a night, Caspar was woken up several times by countless different alarm clocks – and all before having to get up for an early flight! This one definitely goes down as one of the most annoying things you could do to somebody!

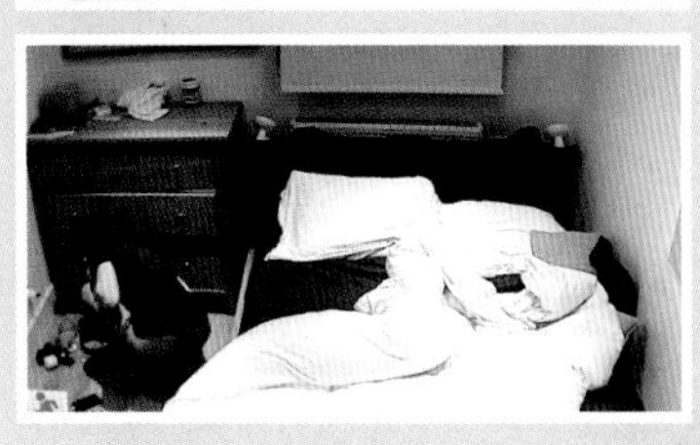

The prank war is never over! Check out Joe and Caspar's channels to see who gets the last laugh.

GAMING GURUS

The gaming industry is big business, so it's no surprise that gaming channels on YouTube are now massively popular, with over half of the world's top channels all belonging to gamers! With a huge community of dedicated fans, top gamers play and share their passion for games online, uploading videos packed with play alongs, how-to tips, tutorials, gaming news, reviews and more!

Gaming videos are so successful that YouTube has even launched its own dedicated gaming platform and app. YouTube Gaming is quite similar to Twitch, and is packed with cool gaming videos, trailers and live playthroughs!

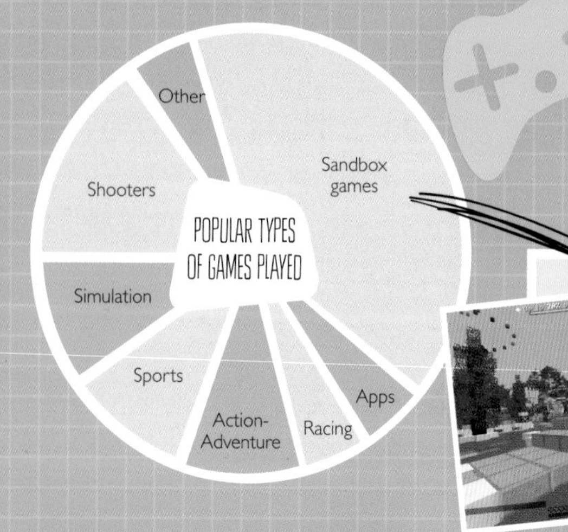

= MINECRAFT!

More people watch YouTube videos about Minecraft than any other game, with Minecraft content making up more than 10% of all of YouTube's daily viewing! Unsurprisingly, gamers who specialise in the blocky game are some of the most successful YouTubers.

Over half of the world's top YouTubers produce 'Let's Play'-style YouTube videos.

LET'S PLAY

>>>>>>>>>>>>>

This is one of the most popular types of video on YouTube. Basically, gamers record themselves playing a game along with a microphone and camera to capture their running commentary and reactions to what's happening on screen. These videos are more fun to watch than just gameplay footage alone, and the big draw is in the YouTube personality playing the game. Let's Plays sometimes feature a few YouTubers playing a game together and usually makes for an entertaining watch, thanks to the fun commentary (gaming and non-gaming related), banter and hilarious reactions, ranging from complete frustration to freaking out!

JUST LIKE: PewDiePie

WALKTHROUGHS

\>>>>>>>>>>>>

Walkthroughs tend to offer more instructional gameplay guides and commentary than 'Let's Plays'. Gamers record themselves playing a game and offer advice and inside information to help the viewer progress in that game, such as tips to complete quests and defeat opponents. Although these videos are generally more educational in nature, they are often still presented in a fun and humorous way.

JUST LIKE: theRadBrad

REVIEWS

\>>>>>>>>>>>>

Review videos are a lot more informative than many other types of gaming video. Here, gamers give an honest opinion on their overall impressions of new video games, letting viewers know exactly what to expect before they decide to buy. Some reviewers make more 'reaction' style reviews, capturing their first impressions and real-time reactions to playing a game for the first time.

JUST LIKE: TotalBiscuit, The Cynical Brit

ANIMATIONS

\>>>>>>>>>>>>

These are possibly the most creative (and, for the creator, time-consuming) type of gaming video. Animations are usually based around a certain game and sometimes use entertaining previous gameplay commentary as the narration. You'll also find hilarious animated parodies, which are often based on popular songs but use gaming characters and themes. Since they are largely based on popular games and current trends, good gaming animations often go viral due to sharing and discussion in the online community.

JUST LIKE: CaptainSparklez

SET-UP STARTER PACK

Want to start your own gaming channel? Aside from your gaming computer or console of choice, here are the things you'll need to produce top-quality content, from the best of the best to the most budget-friendly options.

1. CAPTURE CARD

>>>>>>>>>>>>

The most important thing you'll need to do is record your gameplay! A capture card is a device that connects between your console, your TV and your PC and allows you to capture direct footage rather than using a video camera. It's best to record in HD to stand a chance at success – your videos will look much better quality.

BEST: A good example is the Elgato Capture HD, which is the one used by most major YouTube gamers.

BUDGET: If you're gaming on a PC, you can get totally free game capture software which will do the job, such as the basic version of Fraps.

2. MICROPHONE

>>>>>>>>>>>>

For popular videos like 'Let's Plays' and walkthroughs, audio commentary is a key part of the video. Since your #1 asset is your voice here, you need to ensure that viewers can hear you crystal clear.

BEST: Many YouTubers rate external mics like the Blue Yeti or the Blue Snowball as best for commentary quality, but these can be expensive.

BUDGET: If you already have a gaming headset you can try using the built-in microphone. If not, you can record your voice using a free software programme called Audacity, or there are even free high-quality recording apps for your phone.

PITCH PERFECT

Try to keep your voice engaging when you commentate – speaking in an unchanging monotone is enough to send anyone to sleep.

3. GAMING HEADSET

>>>>>>>>>>>>

Gaming headsets have an integrated microphone, which means you'll be able to communicate with your friends clearly if you're playing a multiplayer game. They also provide excellent surround sound, which is obviously useful for gaming.

BEST: The Astro A40 is one of the best gaming headsets available, with a decent quality microphone that will be good enough to use for YouTube videos.

BUDGET: While headsets are handy for general gaming, if you already have an external microphone you won't really need to buy a fancy headset – there are plenty of decent budget options on the market.

4. EDITING

>>>>>>>>>>>>

Finally, you'll need some editing software to edit and customise your video footage. As a new YouTuber, you need to be brutal with your final edit to avoid videos being too long and to keep your viewer's attention. Aim to turn one hour of game content into around five minutes of footage.

BEST: Sony Vegas Pro is considered to be one of the most advanced editing programmes around. However, it is very expensive, and will probably cost more than the rest of the equipment put together!

BUDGET: Many channels make use of free editing options like Windows Movie Maker, or iMovie for Macs, which will probably have everything you need in the beginning!

Gaming equipment can be super expensive, but you don't need to go out and buy all the best gear before you start making any videos. Even the most successful YouTubers had to start somewhere...

PewDiePie says: "It seems a common misconception that you have to have all these things to get started on YouTube or grow your channel... When I started I had the microphone from my headset and whatever webcam I could find. So, if you're aspiring to make videos really what's stopping you?"

Tom Syndicate saved all his money from his part-time job to buy his gaming and recording equipment. Before that, he says: "I got my dad's camera and stacked it on top of about 20 games on top of the computer and aimed it at the TV – that's how I started."

When jacksepticeye started he simply made the best out of what he had. His top tip? Have fun! "If you're not having fun playing the games, nobody's going to have fun watching you play them! Record games that you really love playing, that you know a lot about... and just do it!"

TOP 10 GAMERS

What could be more fun than playing video games? Watching other, crazier people play them, of course! Whether you want to pick up some great gaming tips, learn about new releases or laugh hysterically at comical commentaries, YouTube's top 10 gamers have got something for everyone.

#10 IHASCUPQUAKE

AKA: Tiffany Herrera

ON YT SINCE: August 2010

KNOWN FOR: Awesome gaming series, animated shorts and collabs with her husband, Red.

Tiffany Herrera, aka Cupquake, has risen through the ranks to become the reigning queen of YouTube female gamers. Cupquake plays a variety of games on her colourful channel, though she is best known for her brilliant series such as 'Minecraft Oasis', her love for singing and her artistic approach to decorating the buildings and houses she makes in games like Minecraft and The Sims.

SUBSCRIBERS • 5.2 MILLION

#9 CAPTAINSPARKLEZ

AKA: Jordan Maron

ON YT SINCE: July 2010

KNOWN FOR: Modded 'Let's Plays', Minecraft music videos and entertaining commentary.

SUBSCRIBERS • 9.7 MILLION

As one of the first YouTubers to start producing high-quality Minecraft content, CaptainSparklez has become a bit of a hero in the YouTube gaming community. His loyal fans love him for his technically advanced worlds as much as his Minecraft music video animations and parodies, which are always entertaining.

#8 THESYNDICATEPROJECT

AKA: Tom Cassell

ON YT SINCE: September 2010

KNOWN FOR: 'Let's Plays' and adrenaline-pumping activities.

SUBSCRIBERS • 9.9 MILLION

Since starting his gaming channel in 2010, Tom has managed to turn his passion for gaming into a full-time career and is now one of the UK's most subscribed-to YouTubers. Syndicate specialises in 'Let's Plays' for the likes of Call of Duty, Halo and Minecraft, always accompanied by his side-splitting commentaries.

#7 JACKSEPTICEYE

>>>>>>>>>>>>>>>>>>>>

AKA: Seán McLoughlin

ON YT SINCE: February 2007

KNOWN FOR: His high-energy 'Let's Plays' and loud personality.

Irish gamer, jacksepticeye, lives up to his claim of being the most 'energetic video game commentator on YouTube' with his high-volume gameplay commentaries on everything from Happy Wheels to GTA V. Jack rose to fame fast after winning a shout-out from the world's most subscribed YouTuber, PewDiePie, gaining over a million subscribers in just one year. Seán is also loved for his 'Reading Your Comments' series and consistent interaction with fans.

SUBSCRIBERS

• 13.6 MILLION

"Top of the morning to ya laddies!"

#6 DANTDM

>>>>>>>>>>>>>>>>>

AKA: Dan Middleton

ON YT SINCE: July 2012

KNOWN FOR: Entertaining adventures in Minecraft, Roblox, Happy Wheels and Pokémon GO.

DanTDM has one of the most highly-viewed channels on YouTube thanks to his huge variety of entertaining gaming content. Whether it's his epic 'Diamond Dimension' survival series, mod showcases, cool mini-games or truly impressive house builds, the dedication that goes into each of Dan's videos is clear to see. With content uploaded daily, there's never a dull moment with DanTDM.

SUBSCRIBERS

• 13.3 MILLION

#5 SKY DOES MINECRAFT

>>>>>>>>>>>>>>>>>>

AKA: Adam Dahlberg

ON YT SINCE: February 2011

KNOWN FOR: 'Let's Plays', random mini-games and crazy Minecraft comedy.

Adam Dahlberg, aka Sky Does Minecraft, has one of the fastest-growing fandoms out there (known as the Sky Army), and for good reason. Though you might not find the most helpful gaming content on this channel, you'll certainly find lots to entertain, with hilarious games commentaries and collabs that'll leave you laughing for hours.

SUBSCRIBERS

• 12 MILLION

Sky originally became popular as part of a Minecraft YouTube team called Team Crafted.

#4 MARKIPLIER

>>>>>>>>>>>>>

Mark is best pals with jacksepticeye, who frequently features in his videos.

AKA: Mark Edward Fischbach

ON YT SINCE: May 2012

KNOWN FOR: Hilarious horror game 'Let's Plays', comedy sketches and parodies.

With his colourful hair, quick wit and awesome gaming skills, Markiplier has quickly made a name for himself as one of YouTube's best-loved gamers. Mark mostly plays survival horror and action video games such as Five Nights at Freddy's, as well as making hilarious comedy sketches, animated parodies and video-game themed musicals!

SUBSCRIBERS	+ 15.7 MILLION

#3 KSI

>>>>>>>>>>>>>>>>>>>>>>>>>>>

AKA: Olajide Olatunji

ON YT SINCE: July 2009

KNOWN FOR: Hyper commentaries and hilarious collabs with his mum and dad.

SUBSCRIBERS	+ 15.2 MILLION

Olajide, otherwise known as KSI, is one of the most hyper gamers on YouTube – and that's saying something! His witty remarks and unique style of commentary have gained him an army of devoted online followers, who tune in to watch his FIFA gameplay, football challenges and comedy sketches.

KSI is set for mainstream success too with movie roles and a rising rap career.

#2 VANOSSGAMING

>>>>>>>>>>>>>>>>>>

AKA: Evan Fong

ON YT SINCE: September 2011

KNOWN FOR: His comedic gaming collabs and funny moments with friends.

Not only is VanossGaming one of the most popular gamers out there, he's actually among the top 20 channels on all of YouTube. If you haven't already heard of him, Evan Fong makes lively 'Let's Plays' featuring games like Grand Theft Auto and Call of Duty, as well as comedy montages and funny collabs with his fellow gaming friends.

SUBSCRIBERS	+ 19.4 MILLION

#1 PEWDIEPIE

>>>>>>>>>>>>>>>>>>>>>>>>>>>>

SUBSCRIBERS

+ 50.8 MILLION

AKA: Felix Kjellberg

ON YT SINCE: April 2010

KNOWN FOR: Hilarious reactions to horror games and one of the most popular personalities on YouTube.

With over 49 million subscribers and 13 billion views, Pewds is the undisputed king of YouTube. Successful for being silly, the Swedish gamer's hilarious facial and vocal reactions to the games he plays have not only made him YouTube's biggest star but also a worldwide celeb, with his own computer game, bestselling book and even a cameo on 'South Park'. A natural trendsetter, PewDiePie is so popular that he has the power to make or break indie video game sales, known as the 'PewDiePie effect', and has even influenced the heart of the industry itself, with developers making new games that are not only fun to play, but fun to watch being played too! Felix's fans are famously known as the 'Bro Army', and can't get enough of his crazy 'Let's Play' videos and unique brand of unfiltered fun.

Pewds started his channel in 2010, and by 2013 he was gaining a new subscriber every second!

Felix was the first YouTube star to exceed 10 billion video views.

Pewds vids often feature his girlfriend, Marzia, or pet pugs, Edgar, Ynk and Maya.

"STAY AWESOME BROS. I KNOW YOU WILL."

IF YOU LIKE THESE, YOU'LL LOVE...

LDSHADOWLADY

STAMPYLONGHEAD

GAMEGRUMPS

YOGSCAST LEWIS & SIMON

ONE TO WATCH: HEYCHRISSA

GAMING BY NUMBERS

Don't be a YouTube noob – brush up on these facts and stats to become a gaming expert.

1

= PewDiePie is the #1 most subscribed channel in the world, beating the likes of Justin Bieber and Rihanna.

36

= The number of years that moustachioed plumber Super Mario has been running round our screens rescuing princesses!

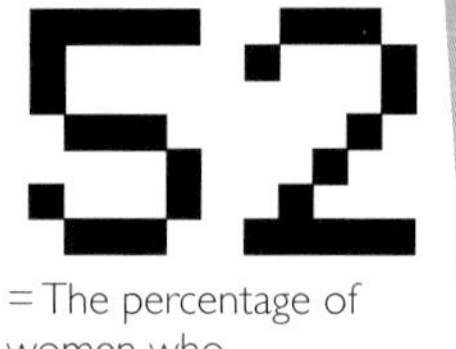

52

= The percentage of women who watch gaming videos on YouTube. Who says girls can't game?!

8·5 MILLION

= The amount of subscribers on gamer Ali-A's channel. This makes his the most popular Call of Duty channel on YouTube.

190

= The record for the most goals scored against the FIFA computer; achieved by top gamer KSI in 2013!

166 MILLION

= The amount of views on CaptainSparklez's Usher music parody '"Revenge" – A Minecraft Original Music Video', making it not only the most-watched Minecraft video ever, but also the most-watched YouTube video for any video game!

2009

= The year the first ever Minecraft video was uploaded to YouTube, by creator Markus Persson. It was called 'Cave game tech test'.

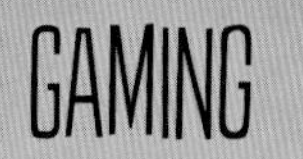

7

= The number of days a week that stampylonghead uploads a new gaming video.

8·4 BILLION

= The amount of lifetime views on DanTDM's channel, making him the second highest viewed gamer on the site (after PewDiePie).

22

= The current number of members in the Yogscast crew – a family of YouTube channels based around gaming.

291

= The average number of minutes that YouTube users spend watching video games a month.

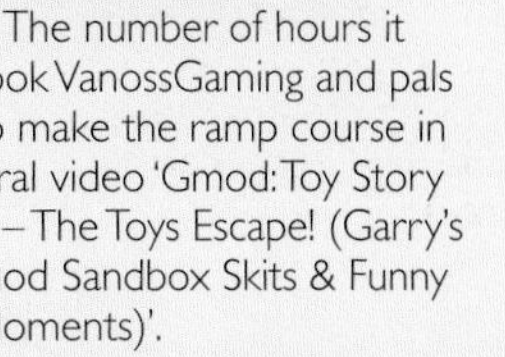

20

= The number of hours it took VanossGaming and pals to make the ramp course in viral video 'Gmod: Toy Story 4 – The Toys Escape! (Garry's Mod Sandbox Skits & Funny Moments)'.

79 MILLION

= Smosh holds the Guinness World Record for the most-viewed fan film based on an adventure game for 'ULTIMATE ASSASSIN'S CREED 3 SONG [Music Video]'. So far it has racked up over 80 million views and was also nominated for a Webby award.

1990

= The year Seán McLoughlin, aka jacksepticeye, was born!

51

= The number of countries that top-selling footie game FIFA is available in.

12 MILLION

= The estimated amount (in dollars) that PewDiePie earned in 2015, making him the highest paid YouTube star in the world.

ADVENTURE TIME!

Ever wanted to travel the globe and have amazing adventures in far-flung destinations? Well now you can! With a whole host of globetrotting vloggers who travel the world and capture it all on camera, YouTube has made it easier than ever to have the world at your fingertips. From extreme adventurers to on-a-budget backpackers, here are just some of the ways they do it.

"Make every day an adventure no matter what you are doing or where you are." – Alex Chacon

EXTREME TRAVEL

>>>>>>>>>>>>

Full of adrenaline pumping activities, adventure, fun and friends, these travel vloggers go to extreme lengths to showcase the exciting side of every destination they visit. There's not much sightseeing or chilling on the beach here – think zip lining, cliff jumping, whitewater rafting, rock climbing and bungee jumping instead! They take risks, push themselves to the limits and have a lot of fun along the way! These channels make for some super fun vicarious viewing and make us want to get out there and live life to max.

JUST LIKE: devinsupertramp, High On Life

GAP YEAR TRAVEL

>>>>>>>>>>>>

Gap years are usually taken either as a break between school and college or between finishing college and starting a full-time job. Whether backpacking, volunteering or working abroad, gap years can be the perfect time to start a travel vlog. As well as documenting their adventures on the road, these vloggers often share their newly-learnt lessons for safe first-time travels – from what to pack to where to go, and how to do it on a budget. Several YouTubers who started a channel during their gap year have even managed to turn their travels into a full time career!

JUST LIKE: Hey Nadine, JacksGap

Successful travel vloggers are able to fund their journeys through sponsors such as hotels, tour companies and tourism boards, as well as any money they make through YouTube.

"Peace out. Enjoy life. Live the adventure." – FunForLouis

DID YOU KNOW? British filmmaker and adventurer Graham Hughes holds the Guinness World Record for being the first person to visit every country in the world – all 201 of them – without using an aeroplane! Graham's shared vlogs of the hardcore four-year adventure on his self-titled YouTube channel.

NOMADIC TRAVEL

>>>>>>>>>>>>>

Nomads, or vagabonds, are long-term travellers who are always moving from one place to another. Instead of having one settled place to live, they call the whole world their home! In YouTube terms, the most successful nomads can travel permanently and get paid for it too. Living out of a backpack is definitely not for everyone, but these channels provide us with non-stop adventures, practical knowledge and travel secrets that can only be gained through years of travel. They share the new countries and cultures they discover, as well as their tips and tricks for a life full of adventure.

JUST LIKE: FunForLouis, Expert Vagabond

TRAVEL TIP If you're not yet old enough to plan a gap year or save enough money, start by filming your family holidays or day trips with friends. Brush up your filming and editing skills and you'll hit the ground running!

"You don't have to travel really far to have an amazing experience." – Alex Ayling, vagabrothers

postcard

Where in the world would you most like to visit?

Wish you were here!

TOP 10 EXTREME GLOBETROTTERS

If you're looking for amazing destinations, travel guides, adrenaline activities and a never-ending supply of adventure inspiration, look no further! These 10 vloggers from around the world take travelling to the extreme, and are on a mission to motivate their viewers to live life to the max.

#10 EXPERT VAGABOND

AKA: Matthew Karsten

ON YT SINCE: July 2011

KNOWN FOR: Vagabonding and taking on adventure activities around the world.

If you're looking for some serious adventure travel inspo, then Expert Vagabond has the videos for you. Matt has been a full-time adventure travel blogger and vlogger for the past six years, sharing crazy stories and useful tips from his non-stop travels around the globe. From mountain trekking in Turkey to scuba diving with sharks in Fiji, Matt's on a mission to inspire his viewers to live a life filled with adventure.

SUBSCRIBERS +11K

#9 ALEX CHACON

AKA: Alex Chacon

ON YT SINCE: September 2010

KNOWN FOR: Motorcycling his way around the world, sharing the journey through epic selfies and 'dronies'.

SUBSCRIBERS +108K

Alex sold everything he owned to undertake an epic journey around the globe, riding his motorcycle across 41 countries in 650 days. Alex shares his creative, one of a kind videos on YouTube, where he's best known for viral videos capturing unique selfies in some of the most stunning locations on earth. He also works with, and donates proceeds from his adventures to charitable causes.

#8 KRISTEN SARAH

AKA: Kristen Sarah

ON YT SINCE: August 2010

KNOWN FOR: Savvy travel tips and adventures off-the-beaten-track.

SUBSCRIBERS +95K

Kristen is a self-confessed travel junkie who loves to jet around the world and explore new places and, thanks to her travel-packed channel, we get to go along for the ride! Kristen's vlogs are energetic, comedic and informative and will take you to parts of the world that most tourists never get to see. This is the channel to inspire adventure seekers everywhere.

#7 VAGABROTHERS

>>>>>>>>>>>>>>>>>>>>>

AKA: Marko and Alex Ayling

ON YT SINCE: October 2013

KNOWN FOR: Exploring and learning about the world through people and culture.

Alex and Marko are explorers through and through. Their mission is to explore the globe, from the biggest cities to the most remote villages, seeking out the people who make each place unique and sharing their stories. The two backpacking brothers got their break on YouTube after they won 'The Biggest, Baddest, Bucket List' video competition, winning the chance to spend six months travelling across six continents carrying out their crazy adventures. The vagabonds have been on the go ever since, so subscribe to join the journey.

SUBSCRIBERS

+144K

#6 SAM EVANS

>>>>>>>>>>>>>>>>>>>>>

AKA: Sam Evans

ON YT SINCE: July 2015

KNOWN FOR: Adventure vlogs with cool vibes, drone shots and on-point editing.

Aussie dude Sam Evans is one of the quickest rising stars in the travel vlogging world, thanks to his crazy, cool vids, artsy edits, fun-loving spirit and collabs with friends like FunForLouis and Zalfie. According to Sam, "life starts at the end of your comfort zone", and it's clear to see that Sam lives life firmly in adventure mode, with short films and vlogs documenting his epic travels around the world and fun times with friends.

SUBSCRIBERS

+132K

#5 HIGH ON LIFE

>>>>>>>>>>>>>>>>>>>

AKA: Parker Heuser, Ryker Gamble and Alexey Lyakh (Rush)

ON YT SINCE: June 2011

KNOWN FOR: Feel-good, crazy and inspirational action-adventure videos.

Parker, Ryker and Rush are three hugely entertaining adventure seekers who post weekly videos inspiring viewers to get out and explore the world. The trio travel to countless countries around the world and do the craziest things imaginable when they get there. From swimming with sharks to skydiving, cliff jumping, volcano boarding and whitewater rafting – the adventures are endless!

SUBSCRIBERS

+310K

WATCH: Ben's 'Visual Vibes' series

#4 MR BEN BROWN

AKA: Ben Brown

ON YT SINCE: October 2006

KNOWN FOR: Stylish vlogs and some serious cinematography skills.

SUBSCRIBERS • 645K

Ben is a former professional kayaker turned filmmaker who treats every day as a new adventure. Whether he's surfing in South Africa, road tripping across California or hanging with mates in a helicopter, Ben's forever up to fun things in cool locations all around the world. Luckily for us he films it all and shares the adventures daily in awesome vlogs filled with fun, friends and positive vibes.

#3 FUNFORLOUIS

AKA: Louis Cole

ON YT SINCE: November 2011

KNOWN FOR: His aspirational daily adventures as a travelling nomad.

SUBSCRIBERS • 1.8 MILLION

It's hard not to be jealous of Louis Cole, who has been able to travel the world for a living by turning his thirst for adventure into a huge online following. Creating slick vlogs from the far-flung corners of the globe, this modern-day explorer makes every day count and loves to inspire his followers to get outside, explore and enjoy life to the max. Louis' travel videos are packed with pals from all over the world, including many top YouTubers.

Louis' adventures often feature his girlfriend and fellow travel vlogger, RayaWasHere.

#2 JACKSGAP

AKA: Jack and Finn Harries

ON YT SINCE: June 2011

KNOWN FOR: Creatively shot, documentary-style stories about their travel adventures.

Jack Harries started his channel as a way to document his gap year adventures and share his love of storytelling with the world. Jack's vlogs soon turned into a full-time job, and after introducing his identical twin, Finn, for the first time on camera, the channel really took off. Whether they're bungee jumping in Thailand, road tripping the width of India in a rickshaw or just turning Jack's bedroom into a giant ball pit, this pair's creative vids are always feel-good and fun.

SUBSCRIBERS • 4.1 MILLION

JacksGap won awards for their filmmaking and directing skills on 'The Rickshaw Run' mini-series.

#1 DEVINSUPERTRAMP

>>>>>>>>>>>>>>>>>>>>>>>>>>

SUBSCRIBERS

+ 4.4 MILLION

AKA: Devin Graham

ON YT SINCE: June 2010

KNOWN FOR: The most amazing adventure and extreme sports videos you'll ever see!

Devin's channel is unlike anything else you'll see on YouTube. After studying film at university, Devin turned his talents to the YouTube world, and now has over 860 million views and multiple viral videos to show for it! A different kind of travel vlogger altogether, Devin is in a league of his own when it comes to making epic adventure videos. As well as always being super high-quality and stunningly shot, his videos are packed with adrenaline-pumping activities, making each upload feel more like a mini action movie! Devin films daredevils and thrill-seekers performing jaw-dropping stunts in some of the most amazing destinations around the world. From wakeboarding in a ravine to a slip and slide 50 ft. off a cliff, Devin always goes the extra mile to make his videos incredible. Definitely a must-subscribe channel for any adventure junkie.

Devin started filmmaking at an early age, breaking several of his parents' cameras in the process!

The name 'Supertramp' comes from the book and movie 'Into the Wild', the story of real life adventurer, Christopher McCandless.

MOST WATCHED VIDEO: 'Assassin's Creed Meets Parkour in Real Life'

"I show the world in a way that no one has ever seen before. I really love what I do. My office has ended up being the world."

IF YOU LIKE THESE, YOU'LL LOVE...

GUNNAROLLA

MIKE COREY

KOMBI LIFE

STEVE BOOKER

ONE TO WATCH: PROJECTONELIFE

EXTREME BUCKET LIST

Are you feeling adventurous? These crazy globetrotters have been busy checking off their bucket list items, one extreme experience at a time! Tick off the bucket list activities you'd be brave enough to try for yourself in the future.

DO A SKYDIVE

>>>>>>>>>

Like JacksGap

- ☐ No way
- ☐ One to try
- ☐ Done!

SWIM WITH SHARKS

>>>>>>>>>

Like Mr Ben Brown

- ☐ No way
- ☐ One to try
- ☐ Done!

BACKFLIP ON A FLYBOARD

>>>>>>>>>

Like High On Life

- ☐ No way
- ☐ One to try
- ☐ Done!

HANG OUT IN A HELICOPTER

>>>>>>>>>

Like FunForLouis and Steve Booker

- ☐ No way
- ☐ One to try
- ☐ Done!

GO DOG SLEDDING

>>>>>>>>>

Like Kristen Sarah

- ☐ No way
- ☐ One to try
- ☐ Done!

GO EXTREME BUNGEE JUMPING

>>>>>>>>>

Like devinsupertramp

- [ ] No way
- [ ] One to try
- [ ] Done!

GO VOLCANO BOARDING

>>>>>>>>>

Like High On Life

- [ ] No way
- [ ] One to try
- [ ] Done!

TAKE A SELFIE IN AN EPIC LOCATION

>>>>>>>>>

Like Alex Chacon

- [ ] No way
- [ ] One to try
- [ ] Done!

TRY WHITEWATER RAFTING

>>>>>>>>>

Like FunForLouis

- [ ] No way
- [ ] One to try
- [ ] Done!

TAKE ON THE WORLD'S TALLEST ROPE SWING

>>>>>>>>>

Like Expert Vagabond

- [ ] No way
- [ ] One to try
- [ ] Done!

Use this space to come up with ideas for your own epic bucket list, full of all the fun adventures and things you want to do during your lifetime.

VLOGGIN' ALL OVER THE WORLD

There's no denying that YouTube is now a global phenomenon, and vloggers come from all four corners of the earth! Check out the map to find the top worldwide web stars sure to spice up your subscription list. We may need subtitles to understand some of them, but one thing's for sure – they're all ridiculously good at producing popular content.

HOLASOYGERMAN.

NAME: Germán Alejandro Garmendia Aranis

NATIONALITY: Chilean

CATEGORY: Comedy

SUBSCRIBERS

+30.4 MILLION

Recently overtaking Smosh to become the second most subscribed-to channel of all time, HolaSoyGerman. is the most famous YouTuber you've never heard of. Germán has attracted many Spanish-speaking fans thanks to his comedic takes on everyday issues.

NORMAN FAIT DES VIDÉOS

NAME: Norman Thavaud

NATIONALITY: French

CATEGORY: Comedy

SUBSCRIBERS

+8.2 MILLION

Norman is well known for his short, comic YouTube videos that have helped make him one of the best-loved vloggers in France. Amazingly, every single one of his videos has been viewed several million times!

SHAAANXO

NAME: Shannon Harris

NATIONALITY: New Zealander

CATEGORY: Beauty

SUBSCRIBERS

+2.8 MILLION

Shannon is New Zealand's #1 YouTube star. A self-confessed beauty junkie, she specialises in sharing her make-up tips, tutorials and reviews online.

WEREVERTUMORRO

NAME: Gabriel Gutierrez Montiel
NATIONALITY: Mexican
CATEGORY: Entertainment

Gabriel, aka Werevertumorro, is a Mexican footballer as well as a vlogger, who has over 1.7 billion views on his channel and 12 million subscribers. This makes him the second most subscribed-to channel in Mexico, after beauty vlogger Yuya.

FAVIJTV™

NAME: Lorenzo Ostuni
NATIONALITY: Italian
CATEGORY: Gaming

SUBSCRIBERS
+3.2 MILLION

This gaming star shares entertaining 'Let's Plays' of everything from Happy Wheels to horror games. Fajiv is one of the most watched YouTubers in Italy and is known for being the first Italian gamer to pass 1 million subscribers.

THEKATECLAPP

NAME: Katya Trofimova
NATIONALITY: Russian
CATEGORY: Lifestyle

Kate Clapp (real name Kayta Trofimova) is a famous Russian YouTube and social media star thanks to her vlogs, travel videos and short comedy skits.

HIKAKINTV

NAME: Hikaru Kaihatsu
NATIONALITY: Japanese
CATEGORY: Comedy

Although not as well-known in English speaking countries, Hikaru is probably the most famous YouTuber in Japan. His videos contain a mix of beatboxing, vlogs, challenges, product reviews and general silliness. He also has a very popular gaming channel called HikakinGames.

ELRUBIUSOMG

NAME: Rubén Doblas Gundersen
NATIONALITY: Spanish
CATEGORY: Gaming

elrubiusOMG is a popular Spanish YouTube star whose channel consists of gameplays, vlogs, challenges and more. In 2015, Rubén became the first Spanish YouTuber to reach 10 million subscribers.

VIRAL VIDEOS

Thanks to video-sharing websites like YouTube and Facebook, viral videos have become a true Internet phenomenon. From funny fails to classic cat videos, auto-tune remixes to the truly bizarre, there's no way of predicting which videos will spread like wildfire all over the web, but we do know that we just can't stop watching them! Here's our pick of the biggest viral sensations of 2016 – if you haven't shared them already.

1 CHEWBACCA MOM

>>>>>>>>>>>>>>>>>>>>

VIEWS: +164 million **FIRST SHARED ON:** Facebook

On 19th May 2016 Candace Payne went live on Facebook to share a new purchase she was super excited about – a 'Star Wars' Chewbacca mask! The video's description reads, 'It's the simple joys in life…' and Candace had the whole world giggling along with her as she tried out her new toy. Watch the video to see one very happy wookie!

2 THE BUILDING IS ON FIRE!

>>>>>>>>>>>>>>>>>>>>>>>

VIEWS: +7.2 million **FIRST SHARED ON:** YouTube

Michelle Dobyne was interviewed after her apartment block caught fire back in 2012, and her hilarious reaction quickly made her a viral star. Her interview has since been remixed, auto-tuned and even blended with the interview of another viral star, Sweet Brown. The most-viewed version was uploaded in January 2016 by the schmoyoho channel, who gave the video their famous 'Songify' treatment. Listen and we guarantee you won't be able to get the catchy tune out of your head – not today!

With over 2.7 billion views, PSY's 'Gangnam Style' music video is still the most viewed viral video on the Internet.

3 MARIO KART FLASH MOB

>>>>>>>>>>>>>>>>>>>>>>>>

VIEWS: +3.7 million **FIRST SHARED ON:** Facebook

In February 2016, UK pranksters Base37 dressed up as characters from Mario Kart and staged their own epic race around a shopping mall in London, complete with banana peel throwing! The video was shared over 57,000 times on Facebook and helped the base jumping team go viral around the world.

4 ZOMBIE APOCALYPSE PRANK

>>>>>>>>>>>>>>>>>>>>>>>>>>

VIEWS: +22.3 million FIRST SHARED ON: YouTube

In April 2016, Millicent Phillip's brothers hatched a cruel but hilarious plan to prank their little sister after her dental surgery. With cleverly pre-recorded radio announcements they managed to convince Millicent, who was recovering from general anaesthetic, that the zombie apocalypse had arrived. They pack the car and ask Millicent to make important decisions, such as which pet they should take with them, and her reactions are absolutely priceless. To be fair, we think she could totally take on any zombie invasion.

5 T. REX NINJA WARRIOR

>>>>>>>>>>>>>>>>>>>>>>>>>>>

VIEWS: +22 million FIRST SHARED ON: Facebook

The 'Ninja Warrior' course is well-known for being challenging, so when the king of the lizards decided to take on the challenge in June 2016 the footage went viral very quickly. With super short arms and limited vision, viewers were impressed with how well this prehistoric predator did!

7 CAT WATCHING HORROR MOVIE

>>>>>>>>>>>>>>>>>>>>>>>>>>>

VIEWS: +2.5 million FIRST SHARED ON: YouTube

Of course, this couldn't be a list of viral videos without at least one cat video in the mix. Possibly the best of the year comes from Togepi the nine-month-old Tabby-Bengal cat, who is literally all of us when it comes to watching a horror movie. Andrew Parrish filmed his cat's hilarious reactions while watching the classic horror film, 'Psycho'. Finally, the scene gets too much for the scaredy cat and she pegs it away from the television in fright.

6 82-YEAR-OLD SINGS HARD ROCK

>>>>>>>>>>>>>>>>>>>>>>>>>>>

VIEWS: +9.8 million FIRST SHARED ON: YouTube

John Hetlinger took part in 'America's Got Talent 2016' and stunned the judges, the audience and the good people of the Internet with his hard rock cover of Drowning Pool's 'Bodies'. The resulting viral video manages to be hardcore, hilarious and heart-warming all at the same time! John has since performed with the band he covered on stage at the Chicago Open Air festival, making it a dream come true for the 82-year-old rocker.

TOP TIP Research has shown that the best length for a viral video is between 15 seconds and five minutes.

FEELING VINE

YouTube isn't the only platform that sends its users viral. When it launched in 2013, Vine totally changed the video game with its short, shareable six-second clips that play continuously on a loop. This shorter form has encouraged content creators to craft videos in a completely different way to entertain an audience in just six seconds. Here are just some of the ways they do it.

In October 2016 it was announced that Vine would close, but the website would remain online so we can still check out our fave Vines on loop. Luckily many of the stars of Vine upload their content to other social media platforms including YouTube, Instagram and Snapchat. Phew!

COMEDY

>>>>>>>>>>>>

These short clips seem to lend themselves to comedy – nearly all of the top 10 channels appear in the comedy category. Whether it's slapstick, jokes, characters or impressions, these Viners get to the punch line quick, leaving viewers LOLing far longer than six seconds!

JUST LIKE: ThomasSanders, Brittany Furlan, KingBach

Known as 'Music's First Vine Star', singer-songwriter Shawn Mendes went from covering songs on the app to a #1 hit almost overnight!

MUSICAL

>>>>>>>>>>>>

Whether it's beatboxing, in-tune harmonies or creative instrument playing – many talented musicians have found an audience on Vine thanks to their perfect musical loops. What's more, they sound like they never end!

JUST LIKE: Us The Duo, Trench, 80Fitz

SMART

>>>>>>>>>>>>

These Vine channels cram as much information as possible into six seconds, creating lots of bite-sized lessons and transforming the way people learn.

JUST LIKE: Exploratorium, NASA JPL, AstroCamp

CREATIVE

\>>>>>>>>>>>>

These innovative filmmakers use everything from stop-motion to special effects to showcase some of the most unique and creative six-second clips you've ever seen.

JUST LIKE: Zach King, meagan cignoli, AliciaHerber

FAMILY

\>>>>>>>>>>>>>

Mixing adorable kids with comedy, these funny family channels are well worth the follow.

JUST LIKE: BatDad, EhBee.TV, Bottlerocket

MEME-MAKER

Short, fast and catchy – it's no wonder Vine has gone global, with over 100 million active users each month. It's also brought us some of today's biggest Internet trends and phrases, from 'Damn Daniel' to 'eyebrows on fleek'!

Many Viners have YouTube channels too!

QUICK TIPS

Want to be a six-second star? We've got six tips to get you started.

USE MUSIC

Rather than spending time conveying emotions, Viners often let the music do the work for them.

#HASHTAG IT

Hashtags make it easier for other users to find your videos.

BE RELATABLE

Many Vines use everyday situations and problems that we can all instantly relate to and put a funny spin on them.

BE QUICK

You've only got six seconds to tell a story so you'll need to talk fast and edit, edit, edit!

TRENDS

Keep up-to-date with current trends and try to make videos around them. Check out the trending hashtags on the 'Explore' page before you start filming.

GET INSPIRED

Follow other Vine users to get your creative juices flowing – you can start by checking out the most successful Viners over the page...

TOP 10 VINERS

Forget 15 minutes of fame – these stars have gained millions of followers in just six seconds! From comedians to musicians, these are the top ten creators who ruled Vine, making high quality content that viewers want to watch again and again. Look out for them on other social media platforms!

#10 THOMASSANDERS

>>>>>>>>>>>>>>>>>

AKA: Thomas Sanders

ON VINE SINCE: April 2013

KNOWN FOR: Clean, funny and positive comedy.

FIND HIM ON: YouTube as Thomas Sanders

FOLLOWERS + 8.3 MILLION

"Story time!" If you've ever been on Vine, chances are you've come across Thomas hilariously narrating the lives of ordinary people in public. Thomas mixes comedy with social commentary to sum up relatable life moments in just six seconds, from making new friends to mental health. The talented Viner is also known for his incredible singing and impersonation skills – his Stewie Griffin impression is spot on.

Thomas is the second most-viewed Vine creator, with over 7 billion loops!

#9 JOSH PECK

>>>>>>>>>>

AKA: Josh Peck

ON VINE SINCE: April 2013

KNOWN FOR: Being a former teen star turned social media celebrity.

FIND HIM ON: Snapchat as Joshuapeck

FOLLOWERS + 9.1 MILLION

Josh isn't your typical Vine celebrity – you might recognise him from his role on the hit show 'Drake & Josh'. Josh has appeared in lots of TV shows and movies since but really slays on social media where he challenges the 'nice guy' reputation he built up being a former teen TV star.

#8 JERRY PURPDRANK

>>>>>>>>>>>>>>>>>>>>>>>>>>

AKA: Jerry Purpdrank

ON VINE SINCE: March 2013

KNOWN FOR: Comedy videos, impersonating celebs and rapping.

FIND HIM ON: Snapchat as Jpurpdrank

FOLLOWERS + 9.3 MILLION

Jerry's Vine comedy skits cover many aspects of modern-day life; from texting etiquette to fashion dos and don'ts. As well as killing it online, Jerry's also launching a music career, has his own mobile game, is signed up for a TV comedy series and makes longer videos on Facebook, too!

#7 LOGAN PAUL

>>>>>>>>>>>>>>>>>

AKA: Logan Paul

ON VINE SINCE: March 2013

KNOWN FOR: Over-the-top slapstick comedy clips with high production value.

FIND HIM ON: YouTube as TheOfficialLoganPaul

FOLLOWERS
+9.4 MILLION

Logan started off making videos on YouTube, but it wasn't until he turned to Vine that he became a social media megastar! Logan's brand of high-energy comedy involves a lot of goofing around and undertaking silly stunts with his mates. He loves to collab with other Vine stars and even Hollywood royalty, such as Dwayne 'The Rock' Johnson.

Vining runs in the family – Logan's little brother, Jake Paul, has over 5 million followers on the platform!

#6 CAMERON DALLAS

>>>>>>>>>>>>>>>>>>>>>>

AKA: Cameron Dallas

ON VINE SINCE: September 2013

KNOWN FOR: Being the king of social media.

FIND HIM ON: YouTube as Cameron Dallas

FOLLOWERS
+9.6 MILLION

Cameron Dallas is the all-American star taking social media by storm. Check out Cameron's Vine channel for his funny pranks and antics with friends and family as well as super short vlogs. He also makes YouTube vids and has over 16 million Instagram followers too! Cameron has now set his sights on the silver screen – with several movie roles already under his belt, a film career is on the cards.

#5 BRITTANY FURLAN

>>>>>>>>>>>>>>>>>>

AKA: Brittany Furlan

ON VINE SINCE: April 2013

KNOWN FOR: Recurring characters, cute pooches and perfectly timed commentary.

FIND HER ON: Instagram as BrittanyFurlan

Brittany's comedic timing is spot on. With eccentric characters such as her airhead roommate 'Barbie' and cameos from her super-cute dogs, Brittany's constantly keeping her fans laughing. Her comedic abilities have not gone unnoticed by mainstream media either – she's currently involved in a comedy sketch show, which is being produced by Seth Green.

FOLLOWERS
+9.9 MILLION

#4 RUDY MANCUSO

AKA: Rudy Mancuso

ON VINE SINCE: February 2013

KNOWN FOR: Original comedy sketches.

FIND HIM ON: YouTube as Rudy Mancuso

FOLLOWERS + 10.6 MILLION

Rudy combines his talents for music and comedy to make one awesome channel. He is particularly known for using his own background to hilariously mock common stereotypes. As well as playing characters like Spanish Batman, Isaac and the moustachioed puppet Diego, Rudy is equally famous for just being himself. He's also a talented pianist and has collaborated with the likes of Justin Bieber.

#3 LELE PONS

AKA: Eleonora Pons

FOLLOWERS + 11.4 MILLION

ON VINE SINCE: April 2013

KNOWN FOR: Her signature brand of slapstick comedy.

FIND HER ON: YouTube as Lele Pons

Lele Pons has quickly become the most-followed female on Vine, turning her vids from a fun hobby into a full time career. The Venezuelan-born Viner is known for her highly-edited funny videos, which often involve physical comedy and pulling pranks on her family and friends with the catchphrase "Do it for the Vine!" Lele also likes to poke fun at how hilarious unfamiliar Venezuelan customs seem to her American friends.

#2 NASH GRIER

AKA: Nash Grier

ON VINE SINCE: April 2013

KNOWN FOR: Comedy sketches, sporting tricks and silliness.

FIND HIM ON: YouTube as Nash Grier

With a mix of sporting mishaps, bad dancing to songs, his super-cute little sister and commentaries on pop culture, Nash has amassed a huge following for his six-second videos. The teen also has more than 4.8 million subscribers on his YouTube channel and has even co-starred in a movie called 'The Outfield' alongside BFF Cameron Dallas!

FOLLOWERS + 12.8 MILLION

Lele was the first Vine star to reach 1 billion loops. She now has over 8.6 billion – making her the most viewed Viner ever!

#1 KINGBACH

>>>>>>>>>>>>>>>>>>>>>>>>>

FOLLOWERS
+16.2 MILLION

AKA: Andrew Bachelor

ON VINE SINCE: April 2013

KNOWN FOR: Being the most followed person on Vine!

FIND HIM ON: YouTube as BachelorsPadTv

With over 16 million followers, KingBach is the top Viner of all time – making him more popular than famous celebs on the platform such as Ariana Grande and Justin Bieber (who he's also collabed with)! Occasionally inappropriate, but always funny, he rose to fame after being introduced to Vine by his friend and fellow creator, Brittany Furlan. By paying attention to what was popular on Vine and incorporating it into his own unique style of comedy, Bach's followers soon skyrocketed. His six-second videos are a hilarious mix of short skits, jokes and recurring characters, and it's clear to see that KingBach puts a lot of effort into creating his clever comedy vids. He frequently collaborates with other Vine stars and many of his collabs are among the most viewed Vines ever! As well as conquering the world of Vine, Bach has also become a mainstream comedian and actor and starred in several TV shows.

Bach says he almost deleted what was to become one of his most famous Vines – 'But That Backflip Tho' – because he wasn't happy with it.

Though best known for Vine, he also has a YouTube channel – BachelorsPadTv.

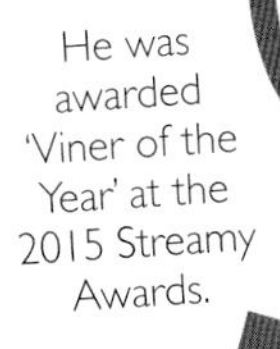

He was awarded 'Viner of the Year' at the 2015 Streamy Awards.

IF YOU LIKE THESE, YOU'LL LOVE...

ZACH KING

US THE DUO

CHRISTIAN DELGROSSO

DAVID LOPEZ

ONE TO WATCH: BIGNIK

PRESS PLAY

YouTube has taken the art of filmmaking from the silver screen to our computer screens; opening the door for aspiring filmmakers of every level. With the opportunity to reach a huge ready-built audience, it's the perfect platform for movie-makers, storytellers and cinefiles to showcase their creative talents. If you're looking for some inspo or simply want to be entertained, these are just some of the film-related videos you'll find.

WEB SERIES

>>>>>>>>>>>>

Instead of watching TV shows, more and more people are now tuning in to web series! These series are mostly scripted, always original and follow a story over a series of episodes. Fresh and exciting, this format allows for a whole lot of creativity. You'll find series that cover a wide range of topics and situations, with unique stories and fresh new talent. Unlike stricter television schedules, web series instalments can be any length, and are usually around five to 10 minutes long.

JUST LIKE: RocketJump – 'Video Game High School', Red vs. Blue, CollegeHumor – 'Jake and Amir'

Filmmakers also upload their work to other platforms such as Vimeo, which is seen by some as the go-to place to post short films and episodic videos.

SHORT FILMS

>>>>>>

Many aspiring filmmakers and established creators showcase their work on YouTube in the form of short films. Not only are they a great way to build an audience but they're also one of the best ways to gain experience and learn the filmmaking craft. You'll find short films of all genres – some are serious and dramatic, some are comedic, some are simply super-creative vlogs! The main point is that they tell a story, and they can do this in anything from five seconds to thirty minutes!

JUST LIKE: 5secondfilms, CaseyNeistat, Bertie Gilbert

PRO TIP: "A good video is 10% idea and 90% execution. A simple idea done well will make for a really good video. If you really want to hone your skills, practice doing one or two minute pieces." – Sam and Niko from Corridor

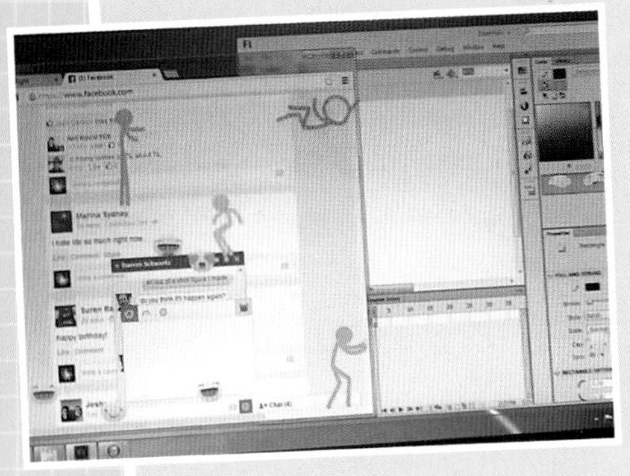

ANIMATIONS

>>>>>>>>>>>>

Whether it's animated short films or cartoon series, animators have always found a huge audience for their work on YouTube. Animation styles vary from stick figures to simplistic cartoons narrating funny stories, sophisticated stop-motion films or complex computer generated imagery. These channels tend to upload less frequently than others, as animation techniques can be very time consuming. A single upload can take anywhere from two weeks to two months, or even two years!

JUST LIKE: Alan Becker, Domics, FilmCow

MOVIE REVIEWS

>>>>>>>>>>>>

Review channels are the best place to keep up-to-date with the latest cinema releases. Reviewers provide their thoughts on everything from first impressions of new releases to the best and worst movies of all time. Some serve up straightforward and serious analysis while others take a more humorous approach; pointing out plot holes and movie mistakes. Entertaining but also educational, review channels often help filmmakers think about the subject on a deeper level.

JUST LIKE: CineFix, Every Frame a Painting, CinemaSins

HOW-TO TUTORIALS

>>>>>>>>>>>>

Looking for some filmmaking guidance and inspiration? Luckily there are lots of tutorial channels that'll show you how it's done! Filled with hours upon hours of tips and advice, they teach everything from screenwriting tips to lighting techniques, camera angles and special effects tutorials. If animation is more your thing, there are lots of channels teaching that too. Who needs to go to film school when you can learn from these experts for free?

JUST LIKE: Film Riot, Indy Mogul, RocketJump Film School

TOP 10 FILMMAKERS

From short films to cinematic vlogs, amusing animations and behind-the-scenes how-tos, YouTube is full of talented filmmakers sharing their stuff with the world. Check out these 10 channels for countless hours of entertaining content on demand.

#10 KICKTHEPJ

AKA: PJ Liguori

ON YT SINCE: October 2007

KNOWN FOR: Insanely creative, quirky short films and crazy characters.

Comedian, musician, vlogger, PJ does it all, though it's in filmmaking where he truly shines, combining slick production values with zany characters to keep his viewers in stitches. His web series 'Oscar's Hotel for Fantastical Creatures' is a must-watch, complete with outlandish monsters and appearances from the likes of gaming megastar PewDiePie!

SUBSCRIBERS: + 1.1 MILLION

#9 ALAN BECKER

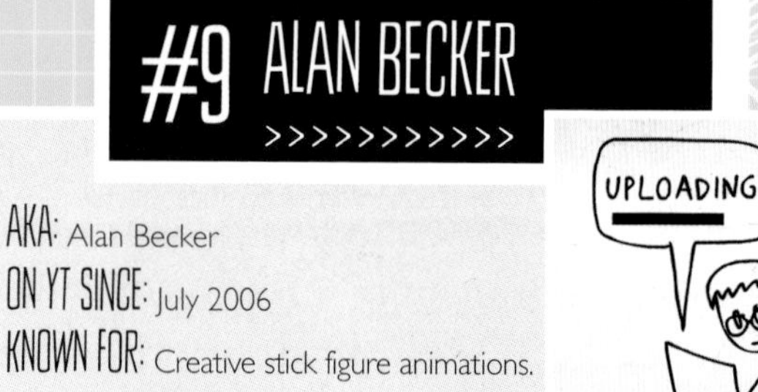

AKA: Alan Becker

ON YT SINCE: July 2006

KNOWN FOR: Creative stick figure animations.

Alan became widely known in 2006 when his viral video 'Animator vs. Animation' exploded. Using nothing but Flash animation, sound effects and amazingly expressive stick figures, Alan tells the story of a stick figure who comes to life and fights against it's creator. Since then, Alan has made several sequels, including the hugely popular 'Animation vs. Minecraft'. He also teaches animation techniques on his second channel, AlanBeckerTutorials.

SUBSCRIBERS: + 2.3 MILLION

#8 THEODD1SOUT COMIC

AKA: James Rallison

ON YT SINCE: August 2014

KNOWN FOR: Entertaining animated stories about his life.

SUBSCRIBERS: + 2 MILLION

James Rallison grew up watching classic YouTube cartoons like 'Charlie The Unicorn' and 'Salad Fingers', and now he's the one inspiring others with his awesome cartoons! A natural storyteller, James shares simple animated videos, talking about everything from annoying roommates to embarrassing moments. As well as his online web comic of the same name, his channel is quickly gaining fans from all around the world.

James started off making comics for his friends at school before turning them into a web comic.

#7 SIMON'S CAT

>>>>>>>>>>>>>>>>>>>>>

AKA: Simon Tofield

ON YT SINCE: November 2007

KNOWN FOR: Animated shorts featuring a very mischievous moggy.

Simon's Cat has become one of the most popular animated series on YouTube, thanks to the hilarious antics of a mischievous white cat and his owner Simon. British animator Simon Tofield uses his four real-life cats as inspiration to perfectly recreate all of the crazy, yet lovable, things that cats get up to, making it a must-subscribe channel for cat owners everywhere!

SUBSCRIBERS

+ 4.1 MILLION

#6 CORRIDOR

>>>>>>>>>>>>>>>>>>>>>>

AKA: Sam Gorski and Niko Pueringer

ON YT SINCE: May 2010

KNOWN FOR: Mind-blowing special effects and cinematic storytelling.

From home-made fan films to YouTube movie magic, best friends Sam and Niko have been making videos together since high school. The pair now produce high-quality video game inspired shorts, from epic live-action Minecraft battles to GTA in real life. Known for their stunning cinematography and special effects, what makes these guys even more impressive is that they make their cinema quality videos on little to no budget – subscribe and prepare to be amazed!

SUBSCRIBERS

+ 4.1 MILLION

#5 TOMSKA

>>>>>>>>>>>>>>>>>>>

AKA: Thomas Ridgewell

ON YT SINCE: May 2006

KNOWN FOR: Funny, random animated videos and action skits.

Thomas 'TomSka' Ridgewell is the British filmmaker currently wowing the web with his action shorts, sketch comedy and cartoons. Tom is best known for the hugely popular 'asfdmovie' series – ultra short cartoons featuring simple characters in hilariously random situations. His channel also features a fair amount of live action content, with well-produced comedy shorts, vlogs and collaborations with other YouTubers.

SUBSCRIBERS

+ 4.2 MILLION

#4 HOW IT SHOULD HAVE ENDED

AKA: Daniel Baxter, Tommy Watson and Christina Alexander

ON YT SINCE: March 2007

KNOWN FOR: Animated alternate endings to popular movies.

SUBSCRIBERS • 6.6 MILLION

If you've ever been left disappointed or baffled by a film ending, How It Should Have Ended are here to put things right. Providing parody alternative endings for some of the most popular movies, they cleverly point out inconsistencies and unexplained plot holes for everything from 'Harry Potter' to 'The Hunger Games'. Check them out for hilarious content, high-quality animations and regular uploads.

#3 ROCKETJUMP

AKA: Freddie Wong, Matt Arnold and Desmond Dolly

SUBSCRIBERS • 7.7 MILLION

ON YT SINCE: February 2006

KNOWN FOR: Creative action vids, special effects and comedy.

Whether it's through TV shows, feature films, comedy shorts or live streams, RocketJump pride themselves on telling great stories and consistently keeping viewers entertained. Well worth a watch is their award-winning web series, 'Video Game High School', which has gained a cult following for its jaw-dropping visual effects and original story. The team also share tutorials, tips and tricks for filmmakers of every level over on RocketJump Film School.

#2 THE SLOW MO GUYS

AKA: Gavin Free and Daniel Gruchy

ON YT SINCE: August 2010

KNOWN FOR: The coolest slow motion channel on the web.

The Slow Mo Guys film pretty much everything in super slow motion, from common challenges to cool stunts, but they're most at home when they're exploding stuff – be that watermelons, water balloons, glass or even Lego! Gavin used to work in the film industry, while Dan has been – you guessed it – an explosives expert in the British army! Check them out for slow mo works of art.

SUBSCRIBERS • 8.7 MILLION

The high-speed cinema camera the guys use is worth a staggering $150,000!

#1 CASEYNEISTAT

>>>>>>>>>>>>>>>>>>>>>>>>>>>>>>

SUBSCRIBERS

+ 6 MILLION

AKA: Casey Neistat

ON YT SINCE: February 2010

KNOWN FOR: Creative, adventurous daily vlogs brimming with style.

He's one of the most imitated filmmakers on the web, but there can only be one Casey Neistat. Casey was making films years before YouTube existed, so brought more than a decade of self-taught videography experience to the vlogging scene. In March 2015, Casey started producing daily vlogs, with the concept of making 'one movie every day', and in doing so totally changed the vlogging game. These creative, high-quality videos took his channel to the next level (he went from 500k to 4 million subscribers in 18 months) and elevated the average vlog into an art form. Casey gives viewers a slice of his incredibly interesting life – whether he's working at his startup, skateboarding through NYC, hanging with family, having lunch with Karlie Kloss or surfing with sharks, every day is a non-stop adventure! His inspiring work ethic and infectious energy make every update addictive to watch. If you're not already a subscriber, start watching now – you won't regret it!

Casey has a huge collection of camera equipment – he uses everything from DSLRs to GoPros, 360s, drones and even his iPhone!

"I try to cut out a small piece of my day and find a story. I make that story the underlining theme of that day's vlog."

Casey is the co-founder of video-sharing app, Beme.

WATCH: 'SNOWBOARDING WITH THE NYPD'

"Creating a new movie every 24 hours and releasing that movie to an audience of hundreds of thousands of people is an evolution in filmmaking."

IF YOU LIKE THESE, YOU'LL LOVE...

NUKAZOOKA

SAWYERHARTMAN

EDDSWORLD

AMI YAMATO

ONE TO WATCH: TONYVTOONS

STORYBOARD IT

Do you fancy yourself as the next big filmmaker? The first step is to get planning! Filmmakers use storyboards to visualise and show how their video will unfold, shot by shot. Plot out your own short scene by drawing in the boxes below.

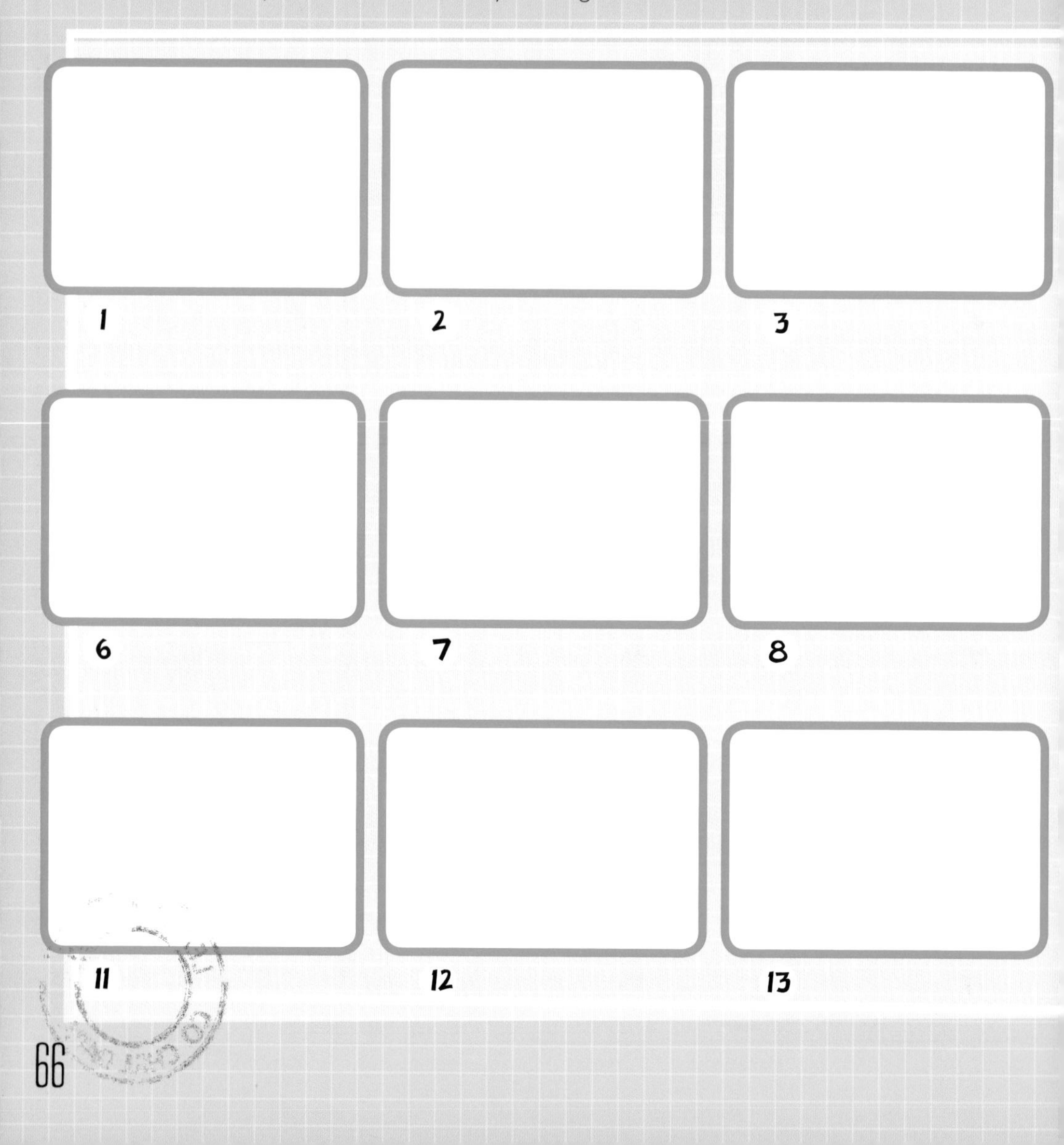

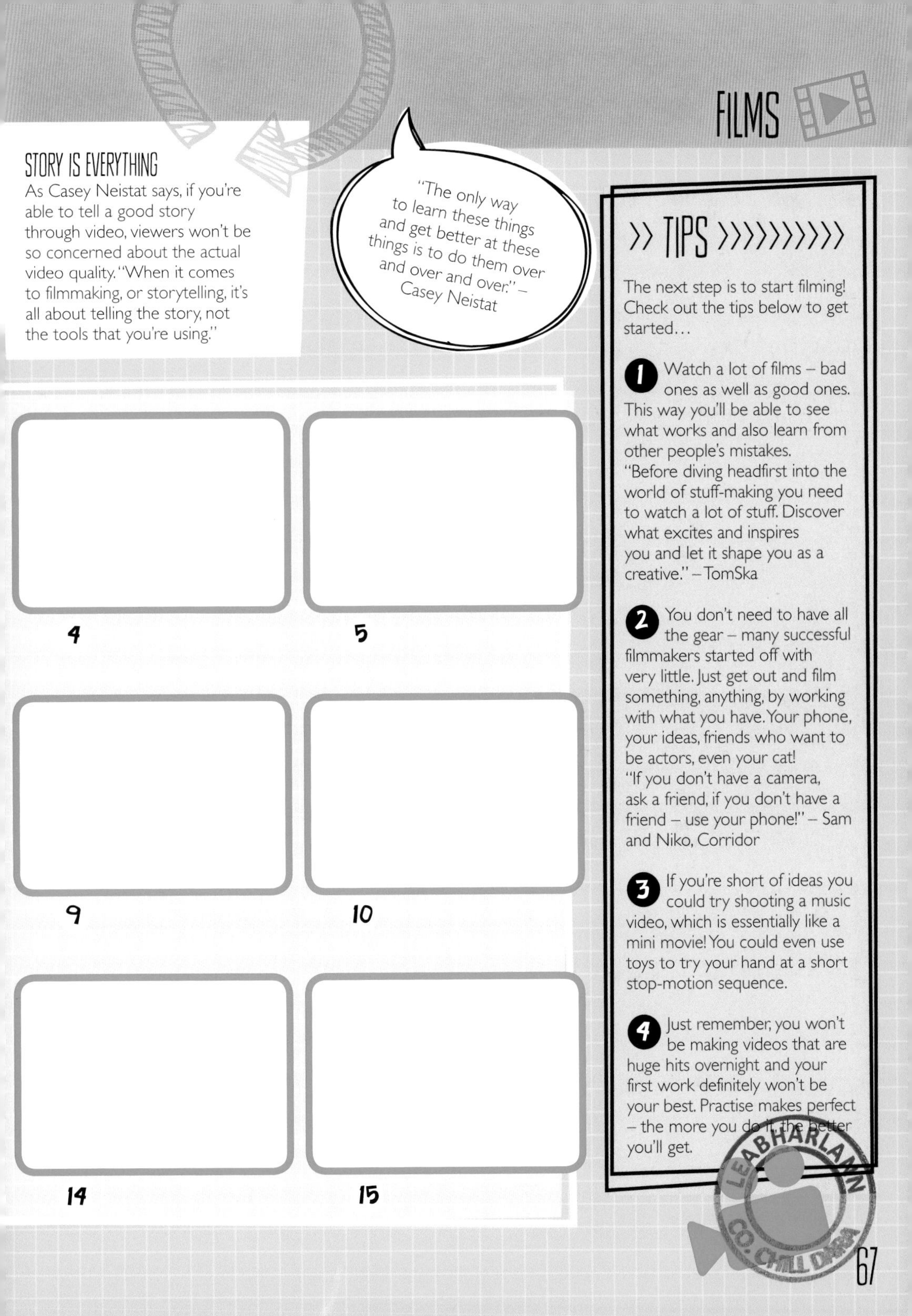

STORY IS EVERYTHING

As Casey Neistat says, if you're able to tell a good story through video, viewers won't be so concerned about the actual video quality. "When it comes to filmmaking, or storytelling, it's all about telling the story, not the tools that you're using."

"The only way to learn these things and get better at these things is to do them over and over and over." – Casey Neistat

4

5

9

10

14

15

>> TIPS >>>>>>>>>>

The next step is to start filming! Check out the tips below to get started...

1 Watch a lot of films – bad ones as well as good ones. This way you'll be able to see what works and also learn from other people's mistakes. "Before diving headfirst into the world of stuff-making you need to watch a lot of stuff. Discover what excites and inspires you and let it shape you as a creative." – TomSka

2 You don't need to have all the gear – many successful filmmakers started off with very little. Just get out and film something, anything, by working with what you have. Your phone, your ideas, friends who want to be actors, even your cat! "If you don't have a camera, ask a friend, if you don't have a friend – use your phone!" – Sam and Niko, Corridor

3 If you're short of ideas you could try shooting a music video, which is essentially like a mini movie! You could even use toys to try your hand at a short stop-motion sequence.

4 Just remember, you won't be making videos that are huge hits overnight and your first work definitely won't be your best. Practise makes perfect – the more you do it, the better you'll get.

YOUTUBE BINGO

Challenge a friend to a game of YouTube bingo the next time you get together for a good old YouTube sesh. See who can be the first to spot these classic things that many YouTubers do!

GAME 1

Vlogger says: "Hi Guys!"	COLLAB VIDEO! (three people or more)	Sponsored video
Video is over 12 minutes long	YouTuber apologises for something at the beginning of the video	You spot fairy lights in the background
Someone pulls a goofy face	CHALLENGE VIDEO!	Vlogger invites viewers to write in the comments section

GAME 1

Vlogger invites viewers to write in the comments section	Vlogger says: "Hi Guys!"	COLLAB VIDEO! (three people or more)
Sponsored video	Video is over 12 minutes long	YouTuber apologises for something at the beginning of the video
You spot fairy lights in the background	Someone pulls a goofy face	CHALLENGE VIDEO!

GAME 2

Someone puts on a funny accent	PRANK VIDEO!	Vlogger asks you to subscribe
There's a cat	Someone sings	There's a non-skippale ad
Video is less than five minutes long	YouTuber is in a different country to you	The vlogger has a cup of tea

GAME 2

PRANK VIDEO!	The vlogger has a cup of tea	Someone sings
Video is less than five minutes long	There's a cat	YouTuber is in a different country to you
There's a non-skippale ad	Someone puts on a funny accent	Vlogger asks you to subscribe

HOW TO PLAY:

- Each player should pick a colour card: red or blue.
- Set up a YouTube playlist to watch.
- Colour or tick off each box when you see or hear these video-related things during the video.
- The first person to get three boxes in a row (horizontally, vertically or diagonally) is the bingo winner.
- If you want to make the game more difficult, check off every box on the bingo card to win!

GAME 3

COLLAB VIDEO! (two people)	Vlogger shows close-up of a product to camera	Vlogger tells you to "Like and subscribe!"
There's an animal on screen	Bloopers reel!	YouTuber has +6 million subscribers
Clickbait video title!	Q&A VIDEO!	Vlogger bursts into song

GAME 3

COLLAB VIDEO! (two people)	Vlogger shows close-up of a product to camera	There's an animal on screen
Vlogger tells you to "Like and subscribe!"	Vlogger shows close-up of a product to camera	Vlogger bursts into song
Q&A VIDEO!	Bloopers reel!	Clickbait video title!

GAME 4

TUTORIAL!	Vlogger reviews a product	Vlogger mentions another YouTuber
There's a dog	COLLAB VIDEO! (with someone of another nationality)	YouTuber has over 10 million subscribers
A relative of the vlogger appears in the vid	ANIMATION!	Vlogger promotes some merchandise

GAME 4

There's a dog	ANIMATION!	COLLAB VIDEO! (with someone of another nationality)
A relative of the vlogger appears in the vid	TUTORIAL!	Vlogger promotes some merchandise
YouTuber has over 10 million subscribers	Vlogger reviews a product	Vlogger mentions another YouTuber

TOP 10 CHALLENGE TAGS

Challenge videos are mega popular, many racking up millions of views and even starting web-wide trends. The idea is to set yourself the most silly/unpleasant/messy/impossible challenge you can think of, and then upload it to the Internet for people to point and laugh at and then do it to themselves. Here are some of the most popular tags to check out or try for yourself, if you dare.

#10 THE DIZZY CHALLENGE

You'll need to spin on the spot repeatedly and then attempt to perform a task while you are – you guessed it – dizzy. Get ready for a lot of laughs and an equal amount of falling on the floor.

WATCH: Joe and Caspar as they dizzily attempt to complete an obstacle course, hold a yoga pose and juggle eggs, with hilarious results. Someone pass Caspar the sick bucket!

#9 THE ACCENT CHALLENGE

The accent challenge started life on 'The Ellen Show' and quickly became a YouTuber favourite. Write down different accents on scraps of paper, and then take turns to choose one and try to talk in that accent whilst the other person guesses.

AUSTRALIAN IRISH

INDIAN FRENCH

ITALIAN CHINESE

#7 THE 'NOT MY ARMS' CHALLENGE

>>>>>>>>>>>>>>>>>>>>>>>>>>>>>

This is a challenge that's MUCH funnier when you fail. The idea here is you wear a large t-shirt with someone else's arms through it, and try to get ready with their hands doing the work instead of yours. Sounds easy, right? WRONG.

#8 THE EGG ROULETTE CHALLENGE

>>>>>>>>>>>>>>>>>>>>>>>>>

Warning: this is guaranteed to get messy. You will need a box of 12 eggs, with eight hard-boiled and four left raw. Take it in turns to pick an egg and immediately crack it on your head. The first person to crack two raw eggs on their head loses. It might sound gross, but it's pretty funny to watch.

You could also try taking turns using one person's legs with the other person's torso for double the fun.

WATCH: Tyler Oakley and SUPERFRUIT team up to take on this ridiculous challenge.

#6 THE 'SAY ANYTHING' CHALLENGE

>>>>>>>>>>>>>>>>>>>>>>

Take turns with a friend in saying random words. If someone stumbles, blanks or repeats a word. the other player gets to apply a piece of sticky tape to their opponent's face. The result is terrifying!

#5 THE WHISPER CHALLENGE

>>>>>>>>>>>>>>>>>>>>

The rules of this game are simple: one person puts on a pair of headphones with loud music blaring and has to guess what phrase the other person is saying by reading their lips only.

#4 THE 'TRY NOT TO LAUGH' CHALLENGE

>>>>>>>>>>>>>>>>>>>>>>>>>>>>>>>

Your opponent takes a huge sip of water, and you try to make them laugh any way you can within 30 seconds. This usually results in them spitting water everywhere, so you'll probably need a change of clothes for this one (unless you're not very funny).

#3 THE TIN CAN CHALLENGE

>>>>>>>>>>>>>>>>>>>>>>

Otherwise known as 'eat it or wear it.' This roulette-type game is for two or more players. Take it in turns to choose an unlabelled can and open it up. Once opened you must either eat a whole spoonful of the content, or smear it on your face – yum! For best results, use a mixture of good and bad cans to build up suspense!

WATCH: Joe and Alfie join forces to attempt the tin challenge, gags aplenty.

#2 THE CHUBBY BUNNY CHALLENGE

>>>>>>>>>>>>>>>>>>>>>>>>>>>>>

This game involves stuffing an alarming amount of marshmallows into your mouth and trying to say the words 'chubby bunny' after each marshmallow. The winner is the person who can fit the most 'mallows in their mouth while still being able to say the words!

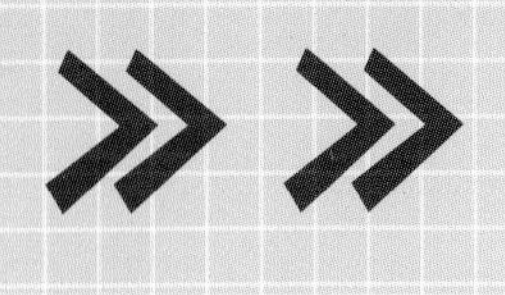

#1 THE 7 SECOND CHALLENGE

>>>>>>>>>>>>>>>>>>>>>>

This popular game is heaps of fun to watch and even more fun to play! Two players take it in turns to give each other absurd tasks which must be completed within seven seconds. Simple! The challenge was invented by YouTuber Phil Lester who came up with hilarious challenges like "sing a song about bricks" and "invent a new dance". There's even a seven second challenge app, with hundreds of challenge suggestions for you to try out.

#NAILEDIT

#FAILEDIT

WATCH: Check out Rhett and Link's 'The YouTube Challenge Challenge' for a mash-up of lots of popular YouTubers competing in loads of challenges all at once! It's the ultimate YouTuber challenge, with milk, make-up, tin cans, baby food and marshmallows galore.

DON'T TRY THIS AT HOME

You may have seen your fave YouTubers trying out these funny challenges and viral trends online, but did you know that some of them could actually be pretty darn dangerous? Here are some of the craziest challenges on the web that may be fun to watch, but you definitely wouldn't want to try them at home.

THE KYLIE JENNER LIP CHALLENGE

>>>>>>>>>>>>

The Internet is full of pictures and videos of people trying to suck their way to a Kylie Jenner pout in this pretty ridiculous challenge. Terrifying outcomes range from swollen fish lips to bruised skin and burst blood vessels – yuck! Bottom line – don't try this at home.

THE CINNAMON CHALLENGE

>>>>>>>>>>>>

One challenge that sounds pretty simple is the Cinnamon Challenge, with everyone from JennaMarbles to PewDiePie swallowing a spoonful of cinnamon without water to see if they can handle it. However, as many have found out the hard way, this challenge is almost impossible to do and harmful too, leading to severe coughing, pain and even the risk of lung damage. The verdict? Sure, this challenge can be fun to watch, but much too dangerous to try at home.

The Cinnamon Challenge is said to have sparked the entire YouTube challenge video trend that's so popular today.

THE MILK CHALLENGE

>>>>>>>>>>>>

Well, this one is just gross. The idea of the milk challenge is to drink an entire gallon of milk in under an hour without throwing any of it back up. It might not sound too bad, but since the human body isn't good at processing that much dairy at once, not to mention the fact that a gallon of anything is more than most people's stomach capacity, the challenge will almost always lead to vomiting. Bleurgh!

MORAL OF THE STORY? ALWAYS USE COMMON SENSE BEFORE TRYING OUT ANY CHALLENGES YOU SEE ON THE INTERNET, AND DON'T TRY THESE ONES AT HOME!

DO GIVE THIS A GO:

YOUTUBER DRAWING CHALLENGE

Grab a mate and take on the YouTuber drawing challenge! Take it in turns to pick one YouTuber and one action from the lists (or come up with your own). Use the space below to draw while the other person guesses. There's just one catch – you'll be drawing blindfolded!

YOUTUBERS	ACTIONS
Miranda Sings	Riding a unicorn
Alfie Deyes	Playing tennis
PewDiePie	Slaying a dragon
Dan and Phil	Eating a hamburger
Louis Cole	Skiing
JennaMarbles	Getting a haircut

PLAYER 1

PLAYER 2

TOP 10 CHALLENGE 'TUBERS

From the chubby bunny challenge to chugging milk, challenge videos have become an essential upload for many YouTubers. This brave bunch of challenge 'Tubers regularly test their limits, team up with each other and take on all kinds of outrageous and hilarious dares, just for our entertainment!

#10 JOSH PIETERS

>>>>>>>>>>>>>>>>>

AKA: Josh Pieters
ON YT SINCE: July 2015
KNOWN FOR: Pranks, exciting challenges and having fun with his YouTube friends.

South African ex-pro cricketer, Josh Pieters, is pretty new to the YouTube world but he's quickly rising up the ranks with his hilarious pranks and challenge videos. Whether he's filming his 'horrendous horse riding', jumping out of a plane or staying awake for 60 hours, there's nothing this adventurous YouTuber won't try.

#9 WHERESMYCHALLENGE

>>>>>>>>>>>

AKA: Harry Ley, Paul Parker, Matthew Collins and Lewis Levy
ON YT SINCE: April 2010
KNOWN FOR: Crazy and gross challenges that most people wouldn't dare to try.

SUBSCRIBERS + 1.2 MILLION

These four British friends take on viewer's challenges and try to beat them, pitting themselves against some truly gross substances, and often failing in spectacular style! Whether they're taking on hot sauce and chilli peppers, rotted fish or worms, viewers love to laugh along at their misfortune.

#8 DOLAN TWINS

>>>>>>>>>>>>>>>>>>>>>>>>>

AKA: Ethan and Grayson Dolan
ON YT SINCE: March 2014
KNOWN FOR: Viral videos, humorous skits and challenges.

SUBSCRIBERS + 2.7 MILLION

Grayson and Ethan are the teenage twins taking the YouTube world by storm. The brothers started out on Vine and made the move to YouTube in 2014, where they took on 'The Blender Challenge' in their very first video. They've been racking up the challenges ever since, with popular videos including a very chilly ice bath challenge and Grayson duct taping Ethan to a door!

#7 OLI WHITE

>>>>>>>>>>>>>>

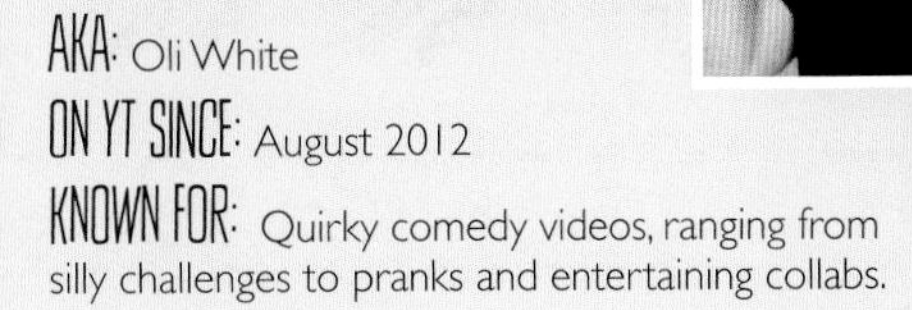

AKA: Oli White

ON YT SINCE: August 2012

KNOWN FOR: Quirky comedy videos, ranging from silly challenges to pranks and entertaining collabs.

SUBSCRIBERS
+ 2.6 MILLION

Oli White is a British YouTuber whose cool combination of challenges, collaborations and funny skits is gaining him fans fast. Oli loves nothing more than to make hilarious videos featuring fellow vlogging friends, family and celebs alike, and uploads entertaining content across his three YouTube channels.

#6 GLOZELL GREEN

>>>>>>>>>>>>>>

AKA: GloZell Lyneette Simon

ON YT SINCE: January 2008

KNOWN FOR: Being the all-time Queen of the challenge video.

SUBSCRIBERS
+ 4.5 MILLION

Green-lipsticked comedian GloZell is known for her wacky personality and ability to take on any challenge, no matter how silly or absurd it may be. With 'cray cray' stunts like her infamous cinnamon challenge viral video, GloZell does everything she can to make her viewers LOL, even if that means sometimes taking it to the extreme!

#5 WASSABI PRODUCTIONS

>>>>>>>>>>>>>>>>>>>

AKA: Alex Burriss

ON YT SINCE: January 2006

SUBSCRIBERS
+ 6.9 MILLION

KNOWN FOR: Funny sketches, parodies and attempting every challenge ever invented.

Alex and Roi Wassabi started out making lip-syncing videos, but found fame thanks to their crazy challenge videos, pushing themselves to the limits by eating all manner of disgusting foods, getting seriously spicy and taking ice baths. Alex now runs the channel solo, and continues to take on any and every entertaining challenge trend, teaming up with all his YouTube friends.

#4 & #3 DAN AND PHIL

>>>>>>>>>>>>

SUBSCRIBERS
+ 6.2 MILLION & + 3.8 MILLION

AKA: Dan Howell and Phil Lester

ON YT SINCE: October 2006 and February 2006

KNOWN FOR: Wacky challenges, comedy skits and awkward stories.

British YouTubing best pals Dan and Phil are known for their quirky sketches, hilarious musings and inventive challenges. The pair united to bring us DanAndPhilGAMES back in 2014, and double up on everything from face swap challenges to doing make-up blindfolded. They are also credited with inventing the immensely popular '7 Second Challenge' and its subsequent app.

Dan has even played the '7 Second Challenge' with Jennifer Lawrence.

#2 MARCUS BUTLER

SUBSCRIBERS
• 4.6 MILLION

AKA: Marcus Butler

ON YT SINCE: January 2010

KNOWN FOR: Wacky challenges, dares, sketches, random musings and his female alter-ego, Margaret.

Drawn to the Internet from an early age, Marcus started out his YouTube career by posting music mixes and edited sports footage online. His comments sections were soon brimming with viewers requesting him to appear on camera himself, so he decided to give it a go and MarcusButlerTV was born! His weekly vlogs are an entertaining mixture of his views on life, hilarious pranks, sketches, challenge attempts and advice, earning him over 4 million subscribers and a whole lot of love.

"HELLOOOOOO!"

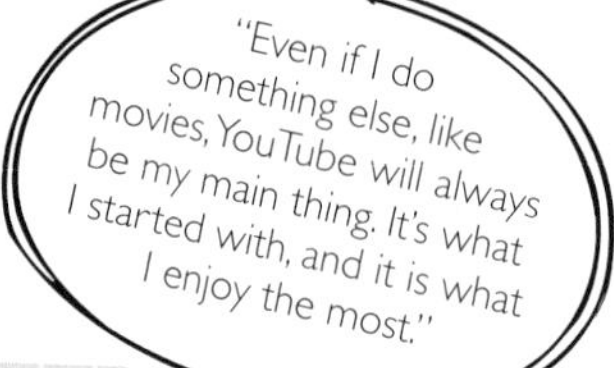

"When I receive hate for doing what I do now, I just think 'that's great', you can hate on me all you want, I'm enjoying what I'm doing."

Marcus has his own cool clothing line, which he sells on his website.

CHALLENGE CHUMS

>>>>>>>>>>>>>>>

It helps to have a great mate to shoot your funny videos with – you'll need someone to hold the camera for you, after all! You never know, you could become the next viral superstars, like this famous pair, otherwise known as 'Malfie'.

Marcus and Alfie met through YouTube way back in 2010. Back then, each had only around 300 subscribers, and decided to meet up because they shared the same passion.

WATCH 'MY OLD MESSAGES TO YOUTUBERS' TO SEE THE FIRST MESSAGES MARCUS EVER SENT TO ALFIE.

Alfie and Marcus quickly became friends and collaborators. These days the pair love nothing better than collaborating on challenge videos together, filming funny sketches, and covering their faces with cream, obvs.

#1 POINTLESS BLOG

SUBSCRIBERS
+ 5.4 MILLION

AKA: Alfie Deyes

ON YT SINCE: July 2009

KNOWN FOR: Pointless challenges, collabs, daily vlogs, silly stunts and lots of laughs.

One YouTuber who manages to take pointless challenges to a whole other level is PointlessBlog's Alfie Deyes. This chirpy Brighton Boy is high in energy and loves to chat, offer advice to his fans, take part in crazy challenges with his mates or simply pull silly stunts like shaving his armpits! His pranks may be slightly pointless, but with two books under his belt, a boatload of loyal subscribers and even his own waxwork model at Madame Tussaud's, Alfie's definitely having the last laugh.

"WHAT'S UP, GUYS?"

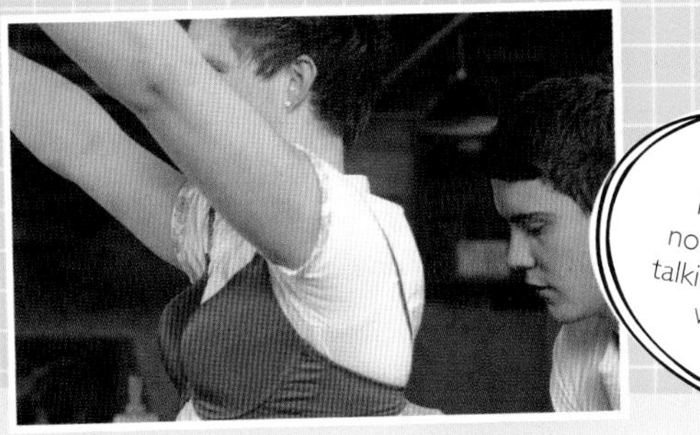

"Keep it real. I'm myself online, I'm not doing an act. I'm just talking to the people who watch my videos."

CHECK OUT:
Alfie's other channels
- PointlessBlogVlogs
- PointlessBlogGames

FACT: Alfie and Marcus hold the world record for a number of challenges they completed together, including 'most bangles put on in 30 seconds by a team of two', and for the 'most number of bras worn and removed by a team of two in one minute', which they achieved with six bras.

They've also broken several Guinness World Records together on the Guinness World Records GWRomg channel, where they were set surprise record challenges to try and complete under the watchful eyes of the Guinness World Record Adjudicators.

Alfie loves to collab on challenge videos with his YouTuber mates including ThatcherJoe, Caspar, Tanya Burr, Sprinkleofglitter, Marcus Butler and of course, girlfriend Zoella. He's even challenged Arianna Grande to do his make-up!

Not all of their challenge attempts have been quite so successful though...

WATCH: '120 CHICKEN NUGGETS IN 20 MINUTES'

RECORD BREAKERS

Fancy being a world record breaker? Pick your challenge, film your attempt and compete with your mates!

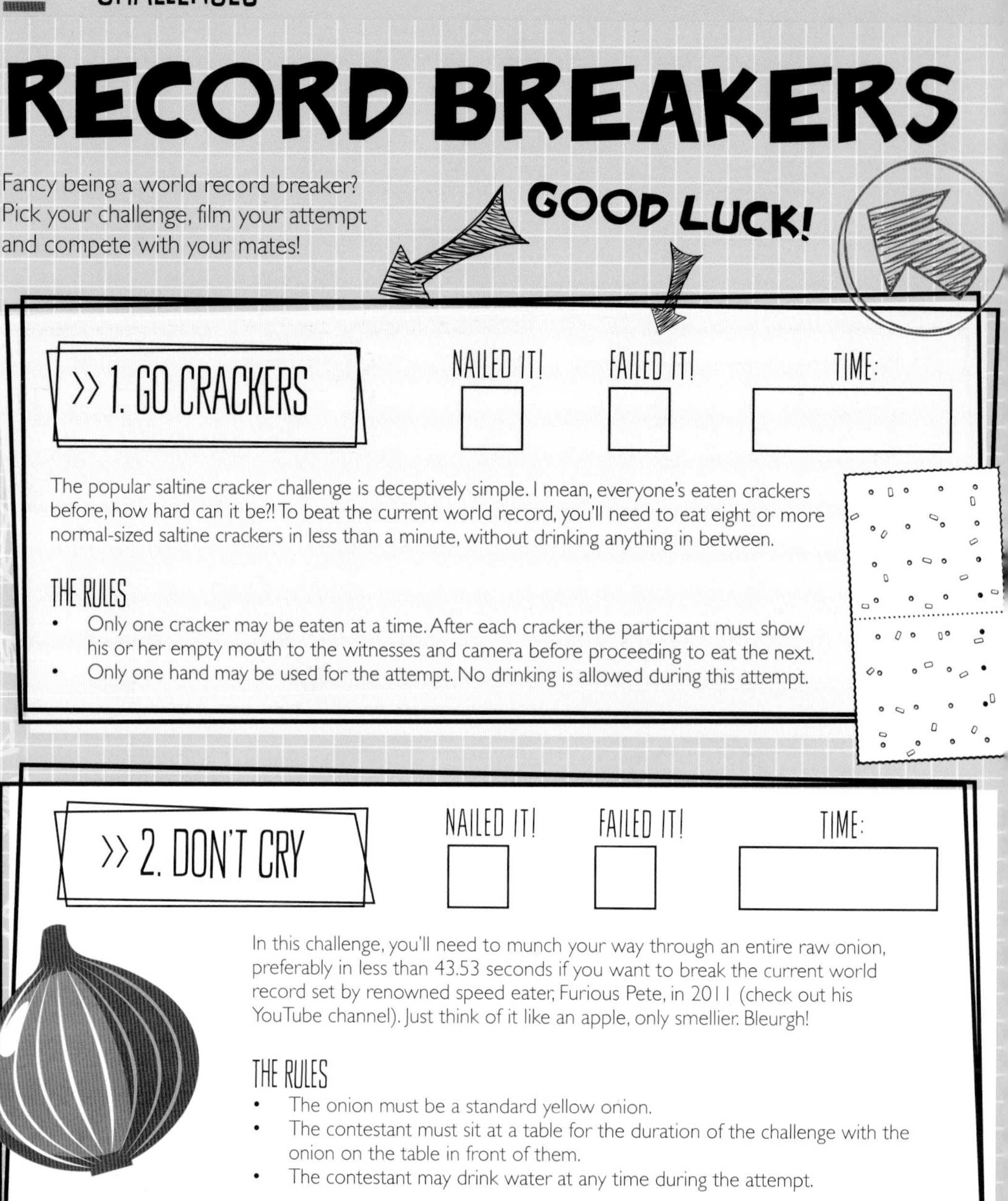

>> 1. GO CRACKERS

NAILED IT! FAILED IT! TIME:

The popular saltine cracker challenge is deceptively simple. I mean, everyone's eaten crackers before, how hard can it be?! To beat the current world record, you'll need to eat eight or more normal-sized saltine crackers in less than a minute, without drinking anything in between.

THE RULES

- Only one cracker may be eaten at a time. After each cracker, the participant must show his or her empty mouth to the witnesses and camera before proceeding to eat the next.
- Only one hand may be used for the attempt. No drinking is allowed during this attempt.

>> 2. DON'T CRY

NAILED IT! FAILED IT! TIME:

In this challenge, you'll need to munch your way through an entire raw onion, preferably in less than 43.53 seconds if you want to break the current world record set by renowned speed eater, Furious Pete, in 2011 (check out his YouTube channel). Just think of it like an apple, only smellier. Bleurgh!

THE RULES

- The onion must be a standard yellow onion.
- The contestant must sit at a table for the duration of the challenge with the onion on the table in front of them.
- The contestant may drink water at any time during the attempt.

>> 3. LOTS OF SOCKS

NAILED IT! FAILED IT! TIME:

The record for the most socks put onto one foot in one minute is 47. Do you have what it takes to 'sock it' to the current world champion?

THE RULES

- Socks used must be standard, commercially-available socks.
- A variation of different sock sizes may be used
- You must start wearing one sock, and this sock won't count towards the tally at the end of the time.

>> 4. READY, SET, TEXT!

NAILED IT! FAILED IT! TIME:

It's easy to write a text message, right? How about writing it blindfolded, without predictive text, and in less than 25.90 seconds? To beat this record, you'll need to type out the following message on a touchscreen phone, without any mistakes, while blindfolded…
The razor-toothed piranhas of the genera Serrasalmus and Pygocentrus are the most ferocious freshwater fish in the world. In reality they seldom attack a human.

THE RULES

- Before the time starts the challenger can hold the phone in either one or both hands but their fingers must not be on the keypad.
- During the attempt the text can be corrected and re-typed.
- Time stops when the challenger (believing the text is completed) holds up the phone at full arm's length.

FUN + FOOD

Dedicated to all things delicious, these channels serve up a whole lot of fun in food form! From calorific concoctions to crazy challenges, there's something to cater to every taste.

>> CRAZY FOOD CHALLENGES >>

FURIOUS PETE

>>>>>>>>>>>>

Furious Pete is a Canadian competitive eater and famous YouTuber with a true talent for eating. He holds six Guinness World Records for eating, including the most hamburgers eaten in one minute and the fastest time to eat a raw onion. Pete documents his record-breaking eating attempts on his channel. From eating 12,000 calories in one sitting to drinking the world's sourest drink; these are the food challenges you definitely wouldn't want to try at home.

SUBSCRIBERS + 3.6 MILLION

WHY NOT TRY THESE FOOD CHALLENGES!

- Chubby Bunny Challenge
- Baby Food Challenge
- Sour Sweets Challenge
- Pancake Challenge
- Chicken Nugget Challenge
- Bean Boozled Challenge

>> NERDY FOOD >>>>>>>>>>

ROSANNA PANSINO

>>>>>>>>>>>>

Rosanna's unique channel combines two different genres – gaming and baking – and clearly she's doing something right because it's the most popular cooking show on the Internet! Rosanna whips up all kinds of themed goodies inspired by characters and objects from video games, cartoons, sci-fi, TV shows, books and films; from Super Mario popsicles to Harry Potter milkshakes.

SUBSCRIBERS + 7.4 MILLION

>> RANDOM FOOD >>>>>>

COOKING WITH DOG

SUBSCRIBERS + 1.2 MILLION

>>>>>>>>>>>>>>>

This channel does exactly what it says on the tin. Cooking with Dog is a Japanese cooking show featuring a dog called Francis and an unnamed female chef. She goes about putting together various dishes while Francis the dog sits next to her and 'narrates' the recipes step-by-step, even when he appears to be sleeping – because why on earth not?!

>> ANIMATED FOOD >>>>>>>>>>

PESFILM

>>>>>>>>>>>>

PESfilm is home to some of the most widely-viewed foody stop-motion films of all time. The creator introduces all kinds of bizarre and imaginative ingredients in films like 'Submarine Sandwich' and 'Fresh Guacamole'. The latter has racked up over 45 million views and is the shortest film to ever be nominated for an Oscar. Probably the most strangely satisfying stop-motion you'll ever see.

SUBSCRIBERS +1 MILLION

>> TINY FOOD >>>>>>>>>>>>>>

HELLODENIZEN

>>>>>>>>>>>>

Featuring tiny animals eating tiny foods, this is probably one of the cutest channels to ever exist. If you've ever wanted to watch a little hamster chomping on a miniature burrito, or a tiny hedgehog having a tiny birthday party complete with a tiny cake, then this is the channel for you!

SUBSCRIBERS +171K

>> GIANT FOOD >>>>>>>>>

HOW TO COOK THAT

>>>>>>>>>>>>

On the other end of the food scale is Ann Reardon's How to Cook That channel. Ann used to be a food scientist and now completes crazy feats of food engineering, making anything from a Minecraft village made out of cake to a whole series of 'Giant Chocolate Bar' tutorials with supersized versions of all your confectionary faves.

>> TASTE TESTS >>>>>>>>>>

EMMYMADEINJAPAN

>>>>>>>>>>>>

Emmy possibly has the best job in the world – eating food for a living! She taste tests foods from all around the world and will literally try anything that her viewers send in to her. From delicious treats to the downright weird, she's sampled candy from almost every country as well as space food, century eggs and even bugs!

SUBSCRIBERS +811K

SPORTING LINEUP

YouTube is home to a huge library of sports channels covering every sport imaginable, from football to free running. Whether you want to watch amazing athletic feats, death-defying stunts, or simply keep up-to-date on all the latest sporting news and scores, there's something to entertain every sports fan.

HEALTH AND FITNESS

>>>>>>>>>>>>>

Thanks to YouTube, you don't need to have an expensive gym membership or even leave the house to get fit and healthy! There are hundreds of online fitness gurus who offer workout routines, recipes and tips for leading a healthy lifestyle.

JUST LIKE: TiffanyRotheWorkouts, blogilates, TheLeanMachines

SPORTS COVERAGE

>>>>>>>>>>>>>

The official YouTube channels for sports leagues, clubs and news networks are the ones to check out to keep up-to-date with your favourite sports. Whether it's player interviews, commentary, recaps, game highlights, analysis or all-access videos, these channels have all the action.

JUST LIKE: NBA, NHL, FIFATV

EXTREME SPORTS

\>>>>>>>>>>>>

This is the place to find thrilling action sports and epic stunts that you're unlikely to see on TV. From adrenaline-filled base jumps to amazing flips, tricks, parkour and freerunning, these channels are sure to get your heart pumping.

JUST LIKE: StuntsAmazing, Red Bull, devinsupertramp

SPORTS CHALLENGES

\>>>>>>>>>>>>>>>>

Mixing sports and comedy can be a recipe for YouTube success. Full of fun, banter and friendly competition, these channels take on all kinds of crazy sports challenges. From competing in crossbar challenges to penalty shootouts, go-kart racing and even doing sports while dizzy, they never fail to entertain.

JUST LIKE: Rule'm Sports, Dude Perfect, Callux

FREESTYLE FOOTBALL

\>>>>>>>>

Football channels are hugely popular all over the world, and those who offer freestyle football are some of the most subscribed. Freestyle footballers perform creative tricks and skills with a football and viewers love to watch it. As well as showing off their insane skills they offer step-by-step tutorials teaching viewers how to pull off some of their top tricks.

JUST LIKE: F2Freestylers, STRskillSchool

TOP 10 SPORTS STARS

YouTube is the perfect platform for sports fans, budding athletes and established stars to show off their skills, and teach others a trick or two while they're at it! These top channels score big on subscribers, producing some of the best sports videos on the Internet.

#10 ADAM LZ

AKA: Adam Lizotte-Zeisler

ON YT SINCE: February 2013

KNOWN FOR: How-to BMX videos – perfect for any BMX beginner.

There's nothing Adam LZ loves more than riding his BMX. With BMX webisodes, how-to tips, tricks and more, Adam's channel is the go-to place for any budding BMX-er. When he's not busy teaching viewers how to do barspins, bunny hops and 360s, Adam's drifting in cool cars with the likes of Roman Atwood or vlogging with his wife Nicole.

SUBSCRIBERS +1.2 MILLION

#9 PROFESSORLIVE

WATCH: 'Spiderman Basketball Part 1'

AKA: Grayson Boucher

ON YT SINCE: November 2009

KNOWN FOR: Superhero basketball series, trick shots and tutorials.

Grayson Boucher, better known as 'The Professor', is an American street basketball player with mad skills. After touring the world and gaining a reputation as an underdog (due to his short stature), he made a name for himself in the sport thanks to his awesome ball handling abilities. His channel features how-to tutorials, highlights and videos that show off his skills. His 'Spiderman Basketball' series has proved to be a slam-dunk success.

SUBSCRIBERS +999K

#8 COPA90

AKA: Various

ON YT SINCE: June 2012

KNOWN FOR: Fun football stories that you won't see anywhere else.

SUBSCRIBERS +1.2 MILLION

The creators behind the British sports channel Copa90 believe that football has the power to unite people from all across the globe. It was created by the fans for the fans, and as a result the channel has been gaining its own loyal fan base ever since its launch. Subscribe for news, top 10s, football animations, interviews and conversations with other fans.

#7 RIDE CHANNEL

AKA: Various pro skaters

ON YT SINCE: February 2011

KNOWN FOR: Daily skateboarding videos.

This is a must-subscribe channel for any skateboarding fan. In association with Tony Hawk's 900 Films Inc. and Complex Media, RIDE Channel showcases the very best of skateboarding. The channel features pro skaters including Tony Hawk, Chris Cole and Jamie Thomas, along with tours, trick tips, how-tos and plenty of hijinks!

SUBSCRIBERS
+1.3 MILLION

#6 RULE'M SPORTS

AKA: Olajide Olatunji (KSI) and co.

ON YT SINCE: June 2014

KNOWN FOR: Top YouTube stars taking on ultimate sports challenges.

The Rule'm Sports YouTube channel features gaming superstar KSI and friends undertaking a whole host of sporting challenges. Tune in to see KSI pushed to the limits as he steps away from his computer screen and onto the sports field. From rugby tackling to penalty shoot outs, Olympic style trampolining to learning how to backflip, KSI tries it all, often with hilarious results.

SUBSCRIBERS
+1.3 MILLION

As well as going head-to-head with fellow YouTubers, KSI is put through the paces by top sports stars such as boxing champion Callum Smith!

#5 BRODIE SMITH

AKA: Brodie Smith

ON YT SINCE: January 2007

KNOWN FOR: Epic frisbee trick shots, tutorials and cool compilations.

Ultimate Frisbee player, Brodie, can throw a frisbee with amazing accuracy. After winning multiple championships, Brodie rose to Internet fame when his 'Frisbee Trick Shots' video went viral. Check out his channel to see him perform epic trick shots all over the world; from dunking discs into a hoop from the other side of a stadium to completing no-look trick shots, cliff jump catches and even throwing to a zip liner as he swings across a gorge!

SUBSCRIBERS
+1.6 MILLION

Brodie holds the Guinness World Record for the furthest frisbee toss into a target.

#4 SKILLTWINS

>>>>>>>>>>>>>

AKA: Jakob and Josef Elzein

ON YT SINCE: April 2011

KNOWN FOR: Their amazing freestyle skills.

SUBSCRIBERS • 2 MILLION

Identical twins Josef and Jakob are two seriously skilled Swedish sports vloggers. The twins have gained millions of views with their easy-to-follow football tutorials, which teach viewers techniques of all kinds, from freestyle skills to famous players' signature moves and FIFA skills in real life. The pair also share funny twin challenges and upload bloopers and fails from their videos.

#3 CALFREEZY

>>>>>>>>>>>>>>>>>>>>>>>>>>>

AKA: Callum Aire

ON YT SINCE: April 2010

KNOWN FOR: FIFA videos, football challenges and bants with mates.

SUBSCRIBERS • 2.8 MILLION

Also known as Cal, this British YouTuber loves football both on the pitch and on the screen. His favourite game is FIFA and he can often be found collaborating with popular gaming group The Sidemen. Cal supports Liverpool F.C., but his friends don't hold this against him! Check him out for footballer interviews, real-life football challenges and fun collabs with other creators such as KSI and W2S.

Calfreezy took on a crossbar challenge at a football match in front of 25,000 people – pressure!

#2 F2FREESTYLERS

>>>>>>>>>>>>>>>>>>

AKA: Billy Wingrove and Jeremy Lynch

ON YT SINCE: April 2011

KNOWN FOR: Amazing freestyle football skills and technique tutorials.

Billy and Jeremy are football mad friends who turned their incredible tekkers into a globally successful YouTube channel. Regarded as two of the best football freestylers in the world, the F2 channel is full of match-play performances, crazy crossbar challenges, football banter and tutorials showing how to pull off the toughest tricks in the game. They've also made videos with some of the world's greatest football players, including Pelé, Messi and Ronaldo.

SUBSCRIBERS • 5 MILLION

#1 DUDE PERFECT

>>>>>>>>>>>>>>>>>>>>>>>>>>>

SUBSCRIBERS

+14.8 MILLION

AKA: Coby and Cory Cotton, Garrett Hilbert, Cody Jones, and Tyler Toney

ON YT SINCE: March 2009

KNOWN FOR: Comedic sports adventures, trick shots and epic battles.

Dude Perfect are five best friends and a panda, who combine sports with comedy. They shot to fame after filming a basketball trick shot video back in 2009. Over 2 billion views and 14 million subscribers later, they are now the #1 sports channel on YouTube! The channel consists of seemingly impossible trick shots and stunts in a wide variety of sports, including American football, ping pong and basketball. The Dudes also compete against each other in epic and unusual sports battles – from racing in lawnmowers to nerf blaster battles and snow sports! Dude Perfect's amazing antics consistently rack up tens of millions of views, and they've also attracted some pretty famous fans too. They collab on videos with star athletes and celebs, including a dizzy sports battle with actor Paul Rudd and tennis trick shots with Serena Williams.

The Dudes have smashed an incredible 11 Guinness World Records! Records include 'Most basketball free throws in one minute by a pair', and 'Longest basketball shot blindfolded'.

The identity of the panda is a mystery!

'Ping Pong Trick Shots 2' has over 81 million views.

Dude Perfect have launched sports game apps and even have their own TV show.

IF YOU LIKE THESE, YOU'LL LOVE...

DAMIEN WALTERS

HOW RIDICULOUS

SEVENGYMNASTICSGIRLS

SCOTTY CRANMER

ONE TO WATCH: THESTEELEJOHNSON

WEIRD AND WONDERFUL

There's no denying that YouTube can be a little bit bonkers, but it's also totally brilliant! We've poked around to bring you some of the silliest, strangest and downright weirdest channels on the web!

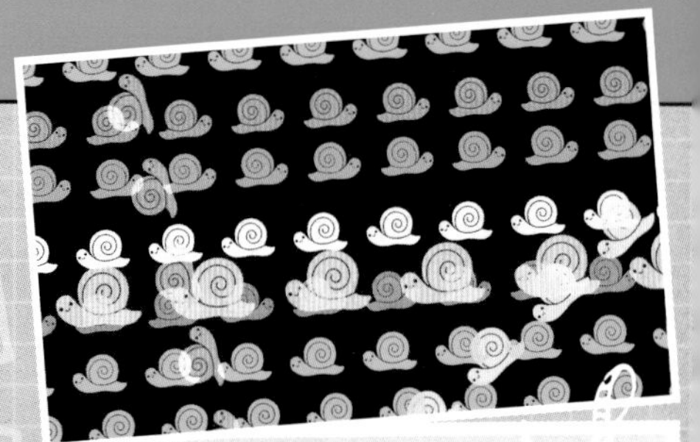

BILL WURTZ

>>>>>>>>>>>>>

bill wurtz creates super-short jingles set to 80s inspired animations. From a surprisingly accurate history of Japan to a two-line song about snails, Bill's bizarre videos are as catchy as they are completely random. Subscribe to be simultaneously confused and amused.

SUBSCRIBERS • 499K

DAVID FIRTH

>>>>>>>>>>>>

David Firth animates things – weird things. The godfather of creepy Internet cartoons, David first rose to fame with his strange and surreal animation series 'Salad Fingers'. Grotesque but brilliant, these are cartoons like you've never seen them before. You have been warned!

SUBSCRIBERS • 731K

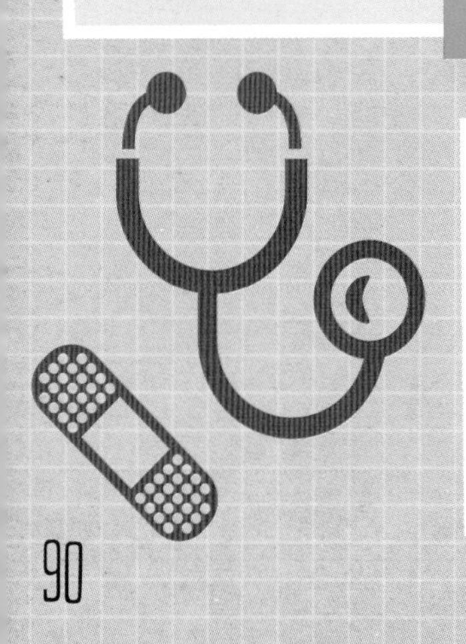

DR. SANDRA LEE (AKA DR. PIMPLE POPPER)

>>>>>>>>>>>>>>>>>>>>>>>>>>>>>>>>>>>>

This channel could well win the prize for the grossest channel on YouTube. Dr. Sandra Lee (aka Dr. Pimple Popper), is a qualified dermatologist whose videos are both medically educational – and disgusting. Weirdly, over 1.9 million people actually subscribe to watch the doctor prod pimples, squeeze cysts and extract all manner of unmentionable things. Bleurgh!

SUBSCRIBERS • 2 MILLION

HOWTOBASIC

>>>>>>>>>>>>

At first glance, HowToBasic looks and sounds just like any other useful how-to channel. However, click on one of the legit-looking thumbnails for a tutorial on 'How To Catch a Pokémon' or 'How To Make Brownies' and they quickly transform into a scene of absolute destruction, with much egg smashing and a whole lot of mess. The anonymous Australian creator quit his job to focus on making videos, 'laying better eggs' and, we assume, a lot of cleaning.

SUBSCRIBERS +8.3 MILLION

FUN TOYS COLLECTOR

>>>>>>>>>>>>

This channel features hundreds of videos of a lady taking toys out of their packaging, and it's insanely popular. With 12 billion all-time channel views, Fun Toys Collector Disney Toys Review has managed to rack up more views than any of your fave YouTubers (king Pewds excepted). Nobody knows who the mysterious toy-unboxer is, but we do know that she's making a whole lot of moolah and getting paid to play all day!

SUBSCRIBERS + 8.6 MILLION

MATTHEWSANTORO

SUBSCRIBERS + 5.6 MILLION

>>>>>>>>>>>>

Canadian YouTuber MatthewSantoro makes entertaining and eye-opening weekly videos featuring the most amazing, funny, mysterious, creepy and little-known facts from around the world. Packed with all kinds of weird and wacky knowledge, this is the place to learn random facts that'll blow your mates' minds.

GRANT THOMPSON

>>>>>>>>>>>>

Known to the Internet as "The King of Random", Grant Thompson's interesting channel is full of cool experiments, crazy life hacks and random projects to try, as well as some some you definitely shouldn't. From making gummy candies to building rockets, turning potatoes into magic mud to instantly freezing drinks; if you enjoy making things that are out of the ordinary, this is the channel for you.

SUBSCRIBERS + 7.3 MILLION

ALL ABOUT THE MONEY

These days, YouTube is no longer just a video watching website, but a legitimate platform for people to earn a living doing something they're passionate about. In addition to making a name for themselves, it's no secret that the biggest YouTuber stars can cash in a lot of money from it...

HOW DO YOUTUBERS GET PAID?

>> YOUTUBE PARTNER PROGRAMME

To make money on their videos, content creators must first become a member of the YouTube Partner Programme. Anyone can become a partner so long as they regularly upload original videos and either own, or have permission to use all of the content in their videos. By making videos monetized, YouTubers receive a share of the income that comes from advertising on YouTube.

>> ADVERTISING REVENUE

These adverts include the skippable and pesky non-skippable ads that play before or during a video, display ads and overlay ads. When it comes to making money from them, it's all about the views! Exactly how much YouTubers get paid per view depends on many factors, such as how many ads were watched or clicked on, the type of advert, what month it is and how many viewers used an ad blocker, because those views won't count.

YouTubers can earn different amounts at different times of the year. December is typically the best month because advertisers spend more money during the Christmas period. This is also why so many YouTubers do vlogmas!

>> MERCHANDISE

Several popular YouTubers also have their own line of merchandise products, which they promote through their channel. From computer games and apps to make-up and clothing, the opportunities are endless. Beyond YouTube, some are also venturing into the world of TV, movies and music, and several have gained lucrative book deals.

By law, vloggers must be upfront and clear with audiences when they have been paid to promote a product, service or brand within a video. This can mean putting the word 'AD' in the title, the thumbnail, or to say it at the start of a video.

>> BRAND SPONSORSHIPS

Popular YouTubers with large audiences can also earn money through sponsorship agreements, which are settled outside of YouTube. Basically, this is where brands pay them to advertise a product to their many subscribers. Sponsorships take many forms, from product placement within a video, to endorsements, giveaways or appearances. The amount of money a YouTuber is offered usually depends on the size of the channel and the amount of 'influence' they are perceived to have, and can range from £100 to £100,000!

YouTube

YOUTUBE RED

>>>>>>>>>>>>>>>>>

Recently, YouTube launched YouTube Red, a monthly-paid subscription service. It provides perks like ad-free videos, watching videos offline and exclusive original shows and movies from top YouTube stars. YouTube Red subscriber views will generate more money for creators, as YouTube shares a percentage of YouTube Red fees just like it does with ad revenue.

» » TOP 10 « «

RICHEST YOUTUBERS

- #10 Nerdy Nummies baker Rosanna Pansino ›› $2.5 MILLION
- #9 Prankster Roman Atwood ›››››››››››››› $2.5 MILLION
- #8 Canadian comedian Superwoman ›››››››› $2.5 MILLION
- #7 Make-up guru Michelle Phan ›››››››››››››› $3 MILLION
- #6 British video game commentator KSI ›››››› $4.5 MILLION
- #5 Funny friends Rhett and Link ›››››››››››› $4.5 MILLION
- #4 Dancing violinist Lindsey Stirling ›››››››››› $6 MILLION
- #3 Web entrepreneurs The Fine Brothers ›››› $8.5 MILLION
- #2 Comedy sketch duo Smosh ›››››››››››› $8.5 MILLION
- #1 King of gaming PewDiePie ›››››››››››› $12 MILLION

Not only did PewDiePie top Forbes' list of the richest YouTubers, but in 2016 he was also named one of 'The World's 100 Most Influential People' by Time magazine. Way to go Pewds!

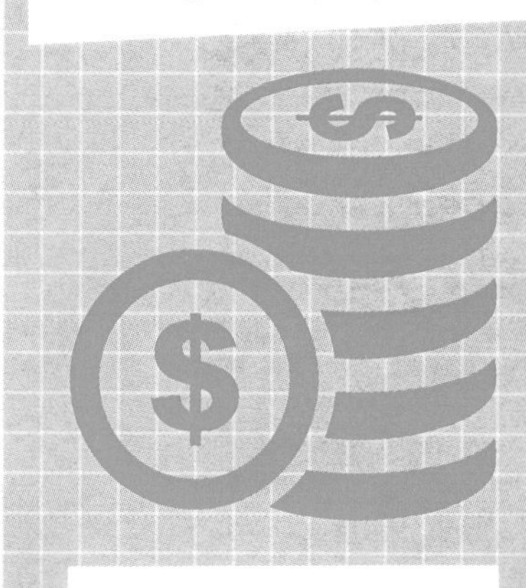

Right, anyone else thinking they should start their own vlogging career...?

YOUR TOP PICKS

You've seen our top 10 lists – now we want to see yours! Fill in each section to create your playlist for ultimate pranks and bants! This doesn't have to be completed all at once – add to the lists as you discover new social media stars and keep track of all your faves in one place.

TOP 5 COMEDIANS
>>>>>>>>>>>>>>>>>>>>>>>

1
2
3
4
5

TOP 5 PRANKSTERS
>>>>>>>>>>>>>>>>>>>>>

1
2
3
4
5

TOP 5 GAMERS
>>>>>>>>>>>>>>>>>>>>>>>

1
2
3
4
5

TOP 5 GLOBETROTTERS
>>>>>>>>>>>>>>>>>>>>>>>

1
2
3
4
5

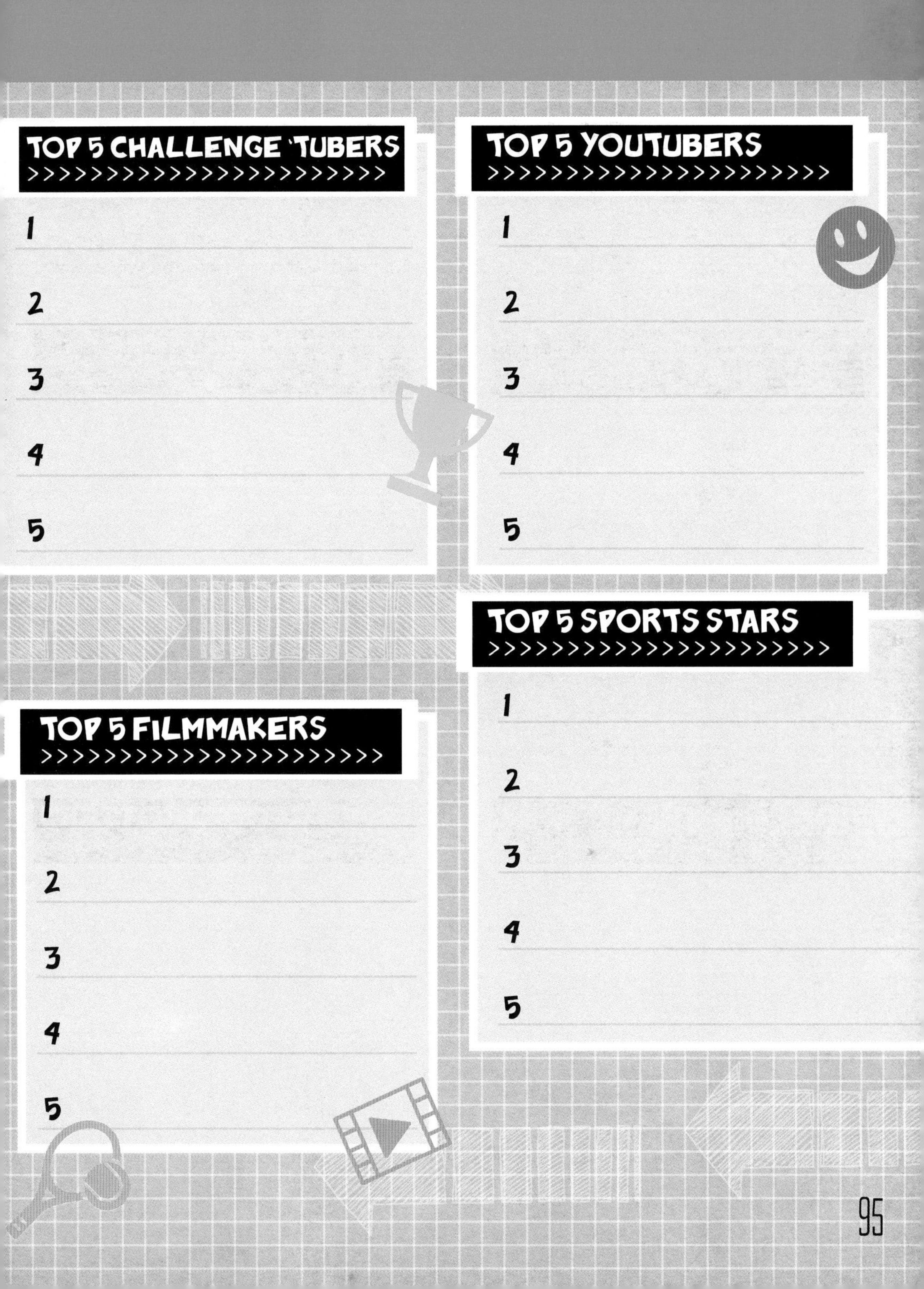

TOP 5 CHALLENGE 'TUBERS
\>>>>>>>>>>>>>>>>>>>>>>>>>>

1

2

3

4

5

TOP 5 YOUTUBERS
\>>>>>>>>>>>>>>>>>>>>>>>>>>>

1

2

3

4

5

TOP 5 SPORTS STARS
\>>>>>>>>>>>>>>>>>>>>>>>>>>>

1

2

3

4

5

TOP 5 FILMMAKERS
\>>>>>>>>>>>>>>>>>>>>>>>>>>

1

2

3

4

5

Picture Credits

...pyright of th.. images remains with the individuals and organisations credited below. Every effort has been made to trace the copyright holders and to obtain their permission for use of copyrighted material. If any accidental omission or error has been made, the publishers will be pleased to rectify this in future editions of this book.

(T = top, B = bottom, L = left, R = right, C= centre)

Cover

TL © PewDiePie/YouTube; TR © TheDiamondMinecart // DanTDM/YouTube; CL © JennaMarbles/YouTube; BL © KSI/YouTube.

Interiors

YouTube: 51TR © ➔FavijTV™/YouTube; 8TR, 60CL © 5secondfilms/YouTube; 86CL © Adam LZ/YouTube; 61TL, 62TR © Alan Becker/YouTube; 4CR, 42TR, 44TR, 49CL © Alex Chacon/YouTube; 20TR © AlishaMarieVlogs/YouTube; 73CR, 73CL © AmazingPhil/YouTube; 53BL © America's Got Talent/YouTube; 65BR © Ami Yamato/YouTube; 20BR © Amplify/YouTube; 9BC © Annoying Orange/YouTube; 15CR © Bart Baker/YouTube; 4BL © Best Viners/Youtube; 29CR © BigDawsTv; 90TR © bill wurtz/YouTube; 15TR © Blimey Cow/YouTube; 87CR © Brodie Smith/YouTube; 53CL © Cabot Phillips/YouTube; 88BL © Calfreezy/YouTube; 33CR, 36TR, 40BL © CaptainSparklez/YouTube; 4BC, 65TL, 65BL © CaseyNeistat/YouTube; 27BL, 30CL, 30BL, 30CR, 30BR, 31TR, 31CR © Caspar/YouTube; 61CL © CineFix/YouTube; 13BL © CollegeHumor/YouTube; 82CR © Cooking with Dog/YouTube; 86BL © Copa90/YouTube; 63BL © Corridor/YouTube; 9CR © crabstickz/YouTube; 89TR © Damien Walters/YouTube; 10TR © danisnotinteresting/YouTube; 77BR © danisnotonfire/YouTube; 74CR © daresundays/YouTube; 90CL © David Firth/YouTube; 47TL, 47BL, 49TL © devinsupertramp/YouTube; 22BR © DmPranksProductions/YouTube; 76BL © Dolan Twins/YouTube; 90BR © Dr. Sandra Lee (aka Dr. Pimple Popper)/YouTube; 89TL, 89BL © Dude Perfect/YouTube; 26BL © Ed Bassmaster/YouTube; 65CR © Eddsworld/YouTube; 21TR © EGX/YouTube; 51BL © elrubiusOMG/YouTube; 83BR © emmymadeinjapan/YouTube; 44BL, 49BL © Expert Vagabond/YouTube; 11TL © extratyler/YouTube; 3C, 4 BR, 7TC, 85BR, 88BR © F2Freestylers/YouTube; 8CL © FailArmy/YouTube; 61BR © Film Riot/YouTube; 14TL © Fine Brothers Entertainment/YouTube; 28BL © fouseyTUBE/YouTube; 91TR © Fun Toys Collector Disney Toys Review/YouTube; 42BL, 46 BL, 48BL, 49CL © FunForLouis/YouTube; 82CL © Furious Pete/YouTube; 39CR © GameGrumps/YouTube; 74C, 77CL © GloZell Green/YouTube; 3C, 13CR, 73BR © Good Mythical Morning/YouTube; 91CR © Grant Thompson - "The King of Random"; 47TR © gunnarolla/YouTube; 79CL, 81TL, 81TC © GWRomg/YouTube; 83TR © HelloDenizen/YouTube; 45CR, 48CR, 49TR © High On Life/YouTube; 51BR © HikakinTV/YouTube; 50CL © HolaSoyGerman./YouTube; 64TL © How It Should Have Ended/YouTube; 89CR © How Ridiculous/YouTube; 83BL © How To Cook That/YouTube; 91CL © HowToBasic/YouTube; 36BL © iHasCupquake/YouTube; 12BL, 16BC © IISuperwomanII/YouTube; 29CR © Improv Everywhere/YouTube; 15 BR © Jack Maynard/YouTube; 35BR © jacksepticeye/YouTube; 37TL © jacksepticeye/YouTube; 15CR © jacksfilms/YouTube; 46BR, 48TL © JacksGap/YouTube; 14BL, 17TR, 72CL © JennaMarbles/YouTube; 76CL © Josh Pieters/YouTube; 4CL © Julien Magic/YouTube; 22TR © Just For Laughs Gags/YouTube; 62BL © KickThePj/YouTube; 47CR © Kombi Life/YouTube; 44BC, 48BR © Kristen Sarah/YouTube; 38BL, 40CR, 72TR, 72CR © KSI/YouTube; 23CR © LAHWF/YouTube; 39 © TRLDShadowLady/YouTube; 23BC © MagicofRahat/YouTube; 38TL, 71TL, 71CL © Markiplier/YouTube; 91BL © Matthew Santoro/YouTube; 29TR © MediocreFilms/YouTube; 47CR © Mike Corey/YouTube; 12CL, 74TR © Miranda Sings/YouTube; 10CL © Mister Epic Mann/YouTube; 46TL, 48CL © Mr Ben Brown/YouTube; 84CL ©NBA/YouTube; 84BR © NHL/YouTube; 8BR, 14BR © nigahiga/YouTube; 9 TL © Noodlerella/YouTube; 50BL © NORMAN FAIT DES VIDÉOS/YouTube; 65TR © Nukazooka/YouTube; 77TL © Oli White/YouTube; 26CR © Ownage Pranks/YouTube; 83CL © PESfilm/YouTube; 4C, 32BL, 35TR, 39TL, 39BL, 40TR © PewDiePie/YouTube; 20CL © Playlist Live/YouTube; 72BC, 72BR © PointlessBlog/YouTube; 6BL © PointlessBlogVlogs/YouTube; 23TL, 29TL, 29BL © PrankvsPrank/YouTube; 86TR © Professorlive/YouTube; 11TR © PsychoSoprano/YouTube; 13TL © Ray William Johnson/YouTube; 27TL © Rémi GAILLARD/YouTube; 4C © Rhett & Link/YouTube; 87TL © RIDE Channel/YouTube; 53BR © RM Videos/YouTube; 60TR, 64BL © RocketJump/YouTube; 28BR © RomanAtwood/YouTube; 82TR © Rosanna Pansino/YouTube; 85CL, 87BL © Rule'm Sports/YouTube; 45BC © Sam Evans/YouTube; 65CR © sawyerhartman/YouTube; 52BL © schmoyoho/YouTube; 89BR © Scotty Cranmer/YouTube; 89CR © SevenGymnasticsGirls/YouTube; 50BR © Shaaanxo/YouTube; 4TL, TR © shane/YouTube; 63TL © Simon's Cat/YouTube; 88TL © SkillTwins/YouTube; 37CR © Sky Does Minecraft/YouTube; 3T, 15TL, 15BL, 41BL © Smosh/YouTube; 18CR © Sophie C./YouTube; 39CR © stampylonghead/YouTube; 47BR © Steve Booker/YouTube; 29BR © Stuart Edge/YouTube; 85TR © StuntsAmazing/YouTube; 18TR © Summer In The City/YouTube; 27CR, 30TR, 30CR, 31CL, 31BL, 31CR, 31BR, 70CL, 70BL © ThatcherJoe/YouTube; 10BR, 11BL, 18BL © ThatcherJoeVlogs/YouTube; 19TR © The DigiTour/YouTube; 9CL © The Key of Awesome/YouTube; 3B, 64BR © The Slow Mo Guys/YouTube; 32CR, 37BL © TheDiamondMinecart // DanTDM/YouTube; 51CR © TheKateClapp/YouTube; 62BC © theodd1sout comic/YouTube; 33TL © theRadBrad/YouTube; 35C, 36BC © TheSyndicateProject/YouTube; 84TR © TiffanyRotheWorkouts/YouTube; 63CR © TomSka/YouTube; 33BL © Total Biscuit, The Cynical Brit/YouTube; 21CL © TURN ON/YouTube; 7CL, 71BL © Tyler Oakley/YouTube; 43TR, 45TC © vagabrothers/YouTube; 6C, 38BR, 41TR © VanossGaming/YouTube; 19CL © VidCon/YouTube; 28TL © VitalyzdTv/YouTube; 73TR, 77CR © Wassabi Productions/YouTube; 51TL © Werevertumorro/YouTube; 76TR © WheresMyChallenge/YouTube; 39BR © YOGSCAST Lewis & Simon/YouTube; 19BR © YouTube FanFest/YouTube; 32TR © YouTube Gaming; 70TR, 71CR © Zoella/YouTube.

Instagram: 78TR © marcusbutler/Instagram; 78BC © marcusbutler/Instagram; 79TR © pointlessblog/Instagram.

Facebook: 53TR © American Ninja Warrior Nation/Facebook; 52BR © Base37/Facebook; 52TR © Candace Payne/Facebook.

Vine: 55TL © BatDad/Vine; 57BR © Brittany Furlan/Vine; 57BL © Cameron Dallas/Vine; 59CR © Christian Delgrosso/Vine; 59BR © David Lopez/Vine; 54BR © Exploratorium/Vine; 56BL © Jerry Purpdrank/Vine; 56TR © Josh Peck/Vine; 59TL, 59BL © KingBach/Vine; 58BL © Lele Pons/Vine; 57TL © Logan Paul/Vine; 58BR © Nash Grier/Vine; 58TL © Rudy Mancuso/Vine; 54TR, 56CL © ThomasSanders/Vine; 54BL, 59CR © Us The Duo/Vine; 55TR, 59TR © Zach King/Vine.

All other images, including YouTube logo courtesy of Shutterstock.com.

Quotation References

17 © AmazingPhil/YouTube; 65 © CaseyNeistat/YouTube; 26 © Ed Bassmaster/YouTube; 42 © FunForLouis/YouTube; 30, 31 © irishexaminer.com; 35, 36 © jacksepticeye/YouTube; 42 © lonelyplanet.com; 78 ©Marcus Butler/YouTube; 47 © mormon.org; 16 © nigahiga/YouTube; 35 © partnersproject/YouTube; 35, 39 © PewDiePie/YouTube; 79 © PointlessBlog/YouTube; 60 © Sam and Niko/YouTube; 15 © Smosh/YouTube; 78 © straitstimes.com; 79 © telegraph.co.uk; 27 © ThatcherJoe/YouTube; 43 © vagabrothers/YouTube; 17 © What's Trending/YouTube.